# Conversations
# Worth Having

# Conversations Worth Having

## Using Appreciative Inquiry to Fuel Productive and Meaningful Engagement

### Second Edition

Jackie Stavros *and* Cheri Torres

Introduction by
David L. Cooperrider

Berrett–Koehler Publishers, Inc.

Berrett-Koehler Publishers, Inc.
1333 Broadway, Suite 1000
Oakland, CA 94612-1921
Tel: (510) 817-2277
Fax: (510) 817-2278
www.bkconnection.com

ORDERING INFORMATION
**Quantity sales.** Special discounts are available on quantity purchases by corporations, associations, and others. For details, contact the "Special Sales Department" at the Berrett-Koehler address above.
**Individual sales.** Berrett-Koehler publications are available through most bookstores. They can also be ordered directly from Berrett-Koehler: Tel: (800) 929-2929; Fax: (802) 864-7626; www .bkconnection.com.
**Orders for college textbook / course adoption use.** Please contact Berrett-Koehler: Tel: (800) 929-2929; Fax: (802) 864-7626.

Distributed to the US trade and internationally by Penguin Random House Publisher Services.

Berrett-Koehler and the BK logo are registered trademarks of Berrett-Koehler Publishers, Inc.

Printed in the United States of America

Berrett-Koehler books are printed on long-lasting acid-free paper. When it is available, we choose paper that has been manufactured by environmentally responsible processes. These may include using trees grown in sustainable forests, incorporating recycled paper, minimizing chlorine in bleaching, or recycling the energy produced at the paper mill.

Library of Congress Cataloging-in-Publication Data

Names: Stavros, Jacqueline M., author. | Torres, Cheri B., author.
Title: Conversations worth having : using appreciative inquiry to fuel productive and meaningful engagement / Jackie Stavros and Cheri Torres.
Description: Second Edition. | Oakland : Berrett-Koehler Publishers, 2021. | Revised edition of the authors' Conversations worth having, 2018. | Includes bibliographical references and index. | Summary: "Conversations can be critical and destructive, or they can be generative and productive. This second edition will help you guarantee that your conversations will allow people, organizations, and communities to flourish"-- Provided by publisher.
Identifiers: LCCN 2021022203 (print) | LCCN 2021022204 (ebook) | ISBN 9781523000104 (paperback) | ISBN 9781523000111 (adobe pdf) | ISBN 9781523000128 (epub)
Subjects: LCSH: Interpersonal relations. | Interpersonal communication. | Appreciative inquiry.
Classification: LCC BF724.3.I58 S728 2021 (print) | LCC BF724.3.I58 (ebook) | DDC 158.2--dc23
LC record available at https://lccn.loc.gov/2021022203
LC ebook record available at https://lccn.loc.gov/2021022204

Second Edition
27 26 25 24 23 22     10 9 8 7 6 5 4 3 2 1

Cover designer: Adam Johnson

For those in conversation

# Contents

## List of Stories

## List of Tables

## List of Figures

# Preface

> *Sometimes the greatest adventure is simply a conversation.*
> *—Amadeus Wolfe*

Conversations lie at the heart of how we interact. We are almost always engaged in either internal dialogue or external interaction. But how often are those conversations worth having? We've heard from countless numbers of people who long for positive change in their lives, communities, and organizations and in the world. They are tired of meaningless interactions and conversations about change that are negative, drag everyone down, and zap energy—and then nothing happens. They are weary of wasting time on conversations that focus on what's wrong, without producing any actionable results. They are frustrated with the destructive conversations broadcast nationally and globally that fray relationships, pit people against one another, and generate fear, distrust, and hopelessness. They long for meaningful engagement that builds connection, fuels productivity, and generates positive change.

This book is about those meaningful conversations. It tells how to have conversations that are productive while strengthening relationships and generating possibilities for a future that works for everyone. Conversations worth having energize people. They foster efficiency, fuel meaningful engagement, and generate creative possibilities. They matter because they inspire collaboration and cooperative action that has a positive impact for individuals, organizations, and communities. We believe that living into our potential begins with these kinds of conversations.

As authors, both of us are longtime practitioners of Appreciative Inquiry (AI), one of the most widely used approaches for fostering positive change in individuals, groups, and organizations. Our journey into AI began in the 1990s when we met David Cooperrider, cofounder of AI. At its core, AI is about discovering the best in people, organizations, and the communities around them. AI is grounded in the notion that we create each moment, and ultimately our social systems, through conversation and shared meaning-making. Appreciative Inquiry is the inspiration of our work as well as the foundation of this book, *Conversations Worth Having*.

In its pages, you will learn two simple AI practices, a strategy to support intentionality, and five powerful principles to make any conversation one worth having. We guide you to ask questions that can change the direction of any conversation, surfacing assumptions, creating shared understanding, building trust, and inspiring connection, new knowledge, and innovation. Rather than heading down a negative path, we show you how to frame conversations in ways that make people you're talking with want to engage and take action. Principles we lay out in the book will influence how you think about your experiences and challenges, helping you reflect on them more constructively and productively. And our technique for tuning in will allow you to be more mindful about who's driving your conversations, increasing your capacity to intentionally foster ones worth having.

We were inspired to write a second edition of the book for several reasons. First, more and more people have been using and sharing the practices from *Conversations Worth Having*. From the first year it was out, there was a request for training and certification in the practices. Since the book was first published in 2018, we've learned a lot about explaining the two AI practices, and we discovered an important factor for success—*tuning in*.

In this second edition, each chapter is still built around real-life stories drawn from our personal and client relationships; some new stories have been added. Each story demonstrates practices and principles that were used to transform both conversations and outcomes. These include primarily applications in the business world, as well as several stories from the realms of education, community change, and family dynamics. Throughout the book, we have improved explanations and clarified concepts to make it easier for people to successfully apply the two practices. This includes clarifying generative questions and offering more examples of using the flipping technique to create a positive frame. At the end of the book, you'll now find generative discussion questions to use for individual reflection (conversations with oneself) and team engagement.

In working with others to apply the practices, we realized a key factor in being successful is our ability to be intentional about our conversations. To support intentionality, we have added a new chapter on tuning in, which is a strategy for recognizing what might be driving our reactions and impacting our interactions. Our work with clients and trainers has taught us that to use these practices effectively, it is important to be aware of our body-mindset and how it is influencing our conversations and well-being. Chapter 3 offers an evidence-based technique for tuning in to your body-mindset. This is a practical way to recognize what's influencing our perceptions, emotions, and thoughts.

In addition, the research in neuroscience, neurophysiology, and positive psychology has continued to grow, adding to the grounded evidence for the efficacy of *Conversations Worth Having,* for individuals, families, organizations, and communities. We have added current research to chapter 7. Finally, we added a discussion guide to support book clubs and teams wishing to take their communication to the next level.

From our vantage point, one of the most exciting things about life is the power of a single conversation to make a significant, positive difference. We invite you to join us in creating a positive change in your life and work by engaging in conversations worth having.

We are on a mission as conversation change agents to share how simple it is to foster conversations that help all people thrive. We are especially grateful to be working with Berrett-Koehler, whose mission is connecting people and ideas to create a world that works for all, and that will happen through conversation. We hope that our contribution to BK's important work will help influence positive change and wellness on the planet. We invite you to be one of many agents who are stimulating conversations to support a world that works for all.

*Jacqueline (Jackie) Stavros*                    *Cheri Torres*
*Brighton, Michigan*                    *Asheville, North Carolina*

jackie@conversationsworthhaving.today
cheri@conversationsworthhaving.today

P.S. Please join our growing community of practice on Facebook, LinkedIn, and Instagram.

# Introduction

> *We live in worlds our conversations create.*
> —David L. Cooperrider

**"I am struck** *by the simple fact that my impact as a leader, and even my whole day, goes better when I share my amazement, when we open minds, live into deeper and better questions, and interdependently emerge new things in every conversation.*

*"Life worth living . . . must be made of affirmation."*

These are the words of one of the most remarkable chief executive officers I've ever worked with, arguably one of the greatest, most thoughtful corporate leaders of modern times. In one of its classic cover stories, *Fast Company* called him the Trillion Dollar Man. The article featured Dee Hock's leadership theory and his founding of Visa, one of the largest, most innovative, and most successful organizations of the past half-century. Today, Visa has a market value of some $446 billion and annual financial transactions approaching $11 trillion.

During Dee's tenure as CEO, the corporation increased its profits by 10,000 percent, but more importantly it reinvented the very concept of organization itself. In many ways, it was an early prototype, not a final model, for the more fully human organization we are seeking and even seeing emerge today. The exciting story in Dee's career is his belief in people, which he expresses this way: "The truth is that, given the right circumstances, from no more than dreams, determination, and the liberty to try, quite ordinary people consistently do extraordinary things."[1]

I had the privilege to work with Dee for more than five years. We were uniting the positive power of Appreciative Inquiry (AI) with his concepts of the more fully human organization—a collaborative, intrinsically motivating system capable of liberating the human spirit without reverting to tired, old command-and-control forms of bureaucracy. After years of working with Dee, I began to search for the core of his success. Yes, he was courageous. True, he was tireless. Right, he was an amazing learner. For example, when I visited his home he had just turned his dining room into a massive library spanning the fields of complexity science through the new biology of living systems to the humanities, including many of the classics in art, history, and literature. There were well over eight thousand titles in that "dining room" library, and each one had his underlines, exclamation points, and margin notes. His insatiable love of learning, of course, was a signature strength. And yes, he was skilled as a CEO, with talents in global finance, negotiations, and the future of digital technologies. Yet I still could not put my finger on his mystery. What was that unique difference, that "something more," that made all the difference and made Dee so extraordinary?

It was not until I opened this *very special and graceful book*, by Jackie Stavros and Cheri Torres, that I understood the secret to that CEO's exceptional career and success. Dee Hock had a gift: a Jeffersonian belief in "we the people" and the idea of "organization as community," which I would summarize as this:

*Our organizational lives and the lives of others flourish or flounder, one conversation at a time.*

For Dee, the difference between success and failure in leadership was all about the art of the "conversation worth having"—precisely the kind that this book describes with such clarity and practicality. Peter Senge, commenting on how Visa was conceived and co-created through literally thousands of conversations and dozens of disciplines, said that the early days of the company "may simply be the best business example of an emerging revolution in organizing."[2]

*Change begins with a single conversation.*

As CEO, Dee Hock instinctively knew that all the abstract notions of management—corporate culture, strategy formulation, organizational alignment, change management, living the brand, joint venturing, winning the customer, enabling innovation, recruiting top talent, creating atmospheres of aspiring versus fearing, improving connectivity, and scaling up excellence—were accomplished one conversation at a time, with teams, persons, and both small and large system meetings. Dee called "this abundance of interdependent diversity that was the deeper meaning." When I look back at our years of working together, what most stands out was how Dee, when at his best, was a maestro of vital conversations—some of the greatest I've ever been part of. Many of them became defining moments. This experience led me to believe this:

> *Every organization and every life's destiny is a series of defin-*
> *ing moments—moments that shape us, change us, and have*
> *a huge impact on our development and strategic choices. Our*
> *research indicates that almost all of these moments involve the*
> *power of vital and caring conversations with significant others.*

After numerous virtual conference calls and telepresence meetings with Dee (not his favorite way of conversing), I recall thinking: "I have never seen a CEO giving so much time and positive energy to each conversation, with such purity of attention, curiosity velocity, and mutual inquiry across boundaries; getting everyone engaged like a contact sport; inviting full voice; and modeling the beginner's mind with real listening. Everyone felt appreciated, honored, elevated, and heard."

In one instance, drawing on lessons from the Visa startup story, we were working with an organization to help its members articulate its body of beliefs, those constitution-like principles that provide the core values for years to come. My job was to apply the mindset of Appreciative Inquiry, an approach that values all voices, seeks to inspire generative theories and possibility thinking, opens our world to new possibilities, challenges assumptions of the status quo, and serves to inspire new options for better living.[3]

Dee called for a conversational process in which a diverse group of all relevant and affected stakeholders would meet and deliberate for three full days, every forty-five days, for an entire year. This schedule provided the time for vital conversations to get at the essence of what matters. Looking back, in a world where relationships are often superficial, this process was astonishing. Because of those inspired conversations, the organization doubled in growth, doubled again, and continues to grow exponentially. So deeply held and valued were its guiding principles that, because of the power of conversations worth having, the organization had the courage to craft one final and concluding principle for the entire global system, with over 850 centers in some 150 countries. This principle stated, "Any individual or organization in this global system can do anything it wants, at any scale, and in any manner—as long as it advances our shared purpose and principles."

This was a radical principle. It asked everyone to be a leader—to build the culture via every conversation. In effect, it told the organization's people that they needed very little traditional supervision. It eliminated the need for a large, expensive, central office hierarchy and thick books on standard operating procedures. It realized that the intrinsic motivation that comes from inspirational beliefs is much more powerful than extrinsic forces. One lesson derived from that principle is highly relevant right now:

> *When you approach each vital conversation as if it could become the most important conversation you might ever have, you can create a positive legacy. How often do we think of our next conversation with this kind of alertness and high anticipation?*

Originally, the prospect of deliberating for three full days, every forty-five days, for twelve months took everyone by surprise. Now, as I look back, I realize it was not the number of days that was important; it was the tough-love message Dee was sending. He was raising the bar on how we conceive of leadership work and think about conversations. In his book that shares the Visa creation story, the word *conversation* is used ten times more than the term *strategic planning.* Conversation is a meeting of hearts and minds. I believe this:

> *When hearts and minds meet, they don't just exchange facts and create atmospheres of hope or despair: they transform them, reshape them, draw different implications from them, engage in new explorations of possibility. Such conversations are literally living systems, living on the edge of chaos and order—like all of life, when it is most alive, busting out all over with pattern and coherence but also alive with novelty and emergence.*

When you think of conversations worth having, think engagement, interweaving, co-creation, inspiration, respect, illumination, emergence, enriched relationships, trust, empathy, and bringing out the best: *think legacy.*

*We live in worlds our conversations create.*

Moreover, leadership is a tapestry of both failed and successful conversations that weave the fine threads of our cultures and relationships, budget alignments, customer communities, innovation trajectories, and best places to work into ethical environments where people can thrive and enable their individual and collective greatness to emerge.

On the reverse side of the tapestry, we've also experienced conversations that have caused irreparable damage—destructive conversations. Consider marriages and partnerships where people wish they could replay history and avoid that one unfortunate and explosive conversation that caused a rupture. Consider another life-depleting form of conversation: the boss who begins every meeting by treating the world or the organization as "the-problem-to-be-solved"; where every agenda item is about threats to the business, failure rates, anger about missteps; and where the main life-depleting atmosphere left in the aftermath is fearful and toxic, some combination of disappointment and distance. And, with all of this at stake— each conversation part of a legacy—recall your schooling. Did you ever take a course on conversations? Not just any kind of conversation, but life-giving ones that serve to open your world to new possibilities, elevate greatness, and build bonds of mutual regard and positive power, not "power over" but "power *to*."

This book, then, represents a breakthrough in the combined fields of Appreciative Inquiry and Peter Drucker–like strengths-based management, positive psychology, and design thinking. What you hold in your hands is the course you've likely never encountered in only one book but always wanted. *Conversations Worth Having* can change your life at work, certainly. Perhaps even more significant, however, is the difference it can make in creating precious, growth-promoting moments and relationships with significant others, family members, partnerships, and community.

Why my excitement? After all, a handful of books out there today describe courageous conversations, confrontational meetings, conflict resolution, and even "ferocious conversations." And while they, too, show how our lives succeed or fail one conversation at a time, I believe this is the *first* book of its kind to take Appreciative Inquiry's profound promise of positive leadership into legacy-creating conversations.[4] Imagine taking the innovation-inspired tools of design thinking, the strengths-based leadership philosophy of Peter Drucker, the science of positive psychology, and the generative power of Appreciative Inquiry for bringing out the best in people and organizations—and then making all of these accessible as the operating system, even the DNA code, inside every conversation worth having.

The possibility that every conversation can start with a positive frame and end in an even more positive way is the central idea of *Conversations Worth Having*. In pursuing this radical idea, the authors take us into the principles of AI, now being applied at places such as Apple, Johnson & Johnson, the US Navy, Coca-Cola, Verizon, Vitamix, Green Mountain Coffee Roasters, and even the United Nations.

For example, instead of the metaphor that "the-world-is-a-problem-to-be-solved"—which almost automatically triggers a deficit-analytic search into breakdowns, gaps, and root causes of failure and places most of our attention on yesterday—we might consider instead an assumption that organizations are living systems, alive, embedded in "universes of strengths." The most vital conversations, this book's authors have discovered, begin in a wide-angle, valuing way—searching *the appreciable world*, which is always larger than our normal *appreciative capacity*, one where the starting assumption is this:

> *It is not only that we live in a universe of strengths and unlimited human imaginations, but surrounding every change situation we are part of—whether internal to the system or external to the system—there exists the strength combinations and innovation potentials, including consciousness shifts, greater than any organizational challenge or opportunity we will ever face.*

Complexity science describes the concept of "sensitive dependence on initial conditions," which can turn tiny snowballs into mountains of avalanches. We see many of those same dynamics in conversations, right from the fateful moment when they are first framed. Small beginnings can have huge consequences, especially in human systems, which often become what those in the system ask questions about most frequently, authentically, systematically, creatively, and rigorously.

So, *Conversations Worth Having* is not at all about turning a blind eye to anything. Instead, it is about something quite artistic, ever so subtle, seeing *beyond the problem* and inviting a different kind of inquiry or search that creates an empowering environment, one that has a high-strengths density and a prospective, future-forming power. You will witness this different kind of inquiry in the first two stories the authors share in chapter 1, about a large teaching hospital and a struggling bank.

This book is built on the authors' relentless optimism, yet it is anything but Pollyannaish. Indeed, in this book, the authors take us into some of the hardest moments any manager, family, business, government, or community might face. *It skillfully provides exactly the right amount of theory for those who want the science of it, but mostly it's about practices you yourself can use and engaging narratives that illustrate and vivify.* The storytelling is honest, heartfelt, and real. You cannot help but reflect on your own life as the authors narrate their own and other transformations.

If you read nothing else, turn to the end of the book for the gripping account of the daughter of one of the authors: it's the true story of a mother and daughter and their response to a young father's harsh and untimely diagnosis of stage four lymphoma. The story, which moved me to tears, was written by the thirteen-year-old daughter, Ally. Courageous Ally teaches us how *Conversations Worth Having* is also about loving and being loved. The bottom line:

*You learn that in any time, any place, any situation, no matter what people tell you, conversations matter and that words, generative questions, and the cognitive power of love—seeing through the gift of new eyes—can change lives, relationships, and organizations.*

If you could choose only one inspiring and resource-rich book on leadership as conversation, what do you suppose it would be? For me, the answer is right here in your hands. Jackie Stavros and Cheri Torres—as well as Ally and her father, Paul—have given us a gift. In business, it will strengthen relationships because the relationship *is* the conversation. In homes and schools, it will help you see and bring out the best in your children and young people—because those, too, are relationships where the conversational ecology is precious and can produce life-defining moments. And when you read this small volume through the lens of your own conversational history, it will likely resonate with something you and many others have experienced:

*Relationships come alive where there is an appreciative eye, when we take the time to see the true, the good, the better, and the possible in each other and our universe of strengths, and when we use this concentrated capacity to activate conversations that open our world to new possibilities, elevate collective genius and purpose, and build bonds of mutual regard and positive power—not "power over" but "power to."*

In the end, Jackie and Cheri have given us the gift of hope. Conversations worth having are those that allow us to grow the most and, in the process, also contribute the most. In a world where so many conversations separate us from our vast potentials, may this book change not simply our world but also the world of conversation.

*Distinguished University Professor, Case Western Reserve University, and Honorary Chair, The David L. Cooperrider Center for Appreciative Inquiry, Champlain College, Stiller School of Business*

# 1

# Shifting Conversations

*One great conversation can shift the direction of change forever.*
—Linda Lambert

**Alisha Patel,** a senior administrator at a thriving medical center in New England, was surprised at the less-than-stellar patient satisfaction report that was sitting on her desk. Her surprise turned to understanding when she saw which hospital unit this was from. The nurse manager of that unit had recently quit because she felt frustrated with the new leadership model and refused to change. Alisha was filling in until a new manager was hired.

She sent a copy of the patient satisfaction report to the nurses in the unit. She also emailed them an assignment for their next staff meeting, which was a week away: "Pay attention. Look for what staff members are doing that contributes to patient satisfaction. Come prepared to share a story of a best practice you've seen during the week."

The nurses were confused when they got the email; one even wrote back, asking if Alisha had made a mistake. "No," she replied, "please look for what's working well and bring your best story next week." This was a dramatic shift from what these nurses were used to, and it created quite a buzz. The former manager usually read them the riot act, tried to find who was at fault, and demanded they do better, or else. They were glad to see her go!

When the nurses met, Alisha acknowledged the team for their quality of care and service to patients. Then she asked about their stories. They each shared a story of best patient care and then together analyzed the stories for strengths and replicable practices. They discovered several unique actions, but mostly there were consistent themes for what created high patient satisfaction. The nurses seemed excited about the ideas. "This was an amazing way to handle our problem, Alisha," one of them exclaimed. "I can't tell you how many meetings we've had that focused on this problem, and nothing ever changed. This was so effective. I know things are going to improve after just one meeting with you!" They left the meeting committed to sharing and implementing the best ideas. They were alive with possibilities!

Alisha smiled confidently as the staff left. She was thinking about the changes that had occurred over the last year. She remembered what it had been like working at the medical center before introducing their appreciative leadership model. They had experienced steady growth in patient services over a three-year period, and, based on that growth, the demands on the staff were having a negative impact on performance, which was evident in their quarterly reports. Patient satisfaction had been steadily declining. Decreasing employee engagement was reflected in unplanned absenteeism and lower retention rates, which made matters worse for everyone. On top of that, patient "throughput" was not optimal, which meant the center lacked the beds they needed to serve the people who needed them most.

All of this negatively affected both the bottom line and employee morale. Everyone felt overworked and stressed. She knew the staff were always striving to provide a high quality of care, but the medical center's growth had become stressful, triggering short tempers, a lack of compassion, limited time for patients, and tension among staff and administration.

Alisha had not always been such an affirming leader. She was responsible for quality, and she lived by the quarterly performance reports. When performance stats were up, she didn't worry; it gave her a chance to focus on other responsibilities. She would send the reports to managers, but she never went out of her way to acknowledge them. She took good reports for granted. When performance stats started declining, it was a different story. She gave the reports all her attention. She spoke face-to-face with managers, and her tone was critical: "These reports are not satisfactory. Every quarter it's the same or worse. You've clearly done nothing to improve!"

The managers would defend the results, saying, "We *have* made changes, but we can't do anything when we are understaffed and people don't show up for work. Some of our staff are already working double shifts to cover for other folks!" "I don't want excuses; I want results," she snapped. "We are doing the best we can," a manager snapped back. "Well, you'll have to do better!" Alisha ended the conversation.

The managers always left demoralized and with no ideas about how to resolve the issue. Alisha's levels of stress and dissatisfaction grew over this period, and it became next to impossible to hide her frustration from her colleagues. Her stress rolled over into her family and nonprofessional life as well. She became short-tempered, negative, and quick to criticize both her kids and her husband. She had fast developed a reputation for being the kind of person she never wanted to be as a manager, partner, or parent. She realized she was going to have to do something if she wanted things to change. So she began an online search. She was intrigued by the headline of an upcoming workshop she found, about something called Appreciative Inquiry (AI), which promised tools and strategies for strengths-based change at any level—personal, organizational, and community.[1] What caught her attention was this headline:

> The Best Healthcare Clinics in the World
> Are Strengths-Based; Their Performance
> Outpaces All Others!

She read further: "When we're unable to act with agility, speed, and unity, opportunities are missed, and revenue is lost." It was as if these words were written just for her. In hospitals, she knew, agility and speed can mean the difference between life and death, and lost revenue seemed to lead to financial decisions that negatively affected quality. What convinced her that this was the workshop she needed was a quote from David Cooperrider: "We change best when we are strongest and most positive, not when we feel the weakest, most negative, or helpless."[2] She realized she had become negative, focusing on everyone's weaknesses, including her own. Everyone was feeling helpless to turn things around. So she clicked on the registration tab.

During her training, she learned about the practices and principles of AI. Somewhere in the midst of the week she realized she herself had actually been contributing to the problem at her own medical center. She had dug in her heels and had badgered the staff, without asking any questions or helping to find solutions. She vowed to be part of the solution when she returned.

The first thing she did was to create a positive framework for her next conversation: "More and more, our patients feel highly satisfied with our care." Then she adopted an attitude of curiosity. She wondered if some of the patients were highly satisfied. If they were, why? What were their stories? What were the staff who cared for them doing that made a difference? These were the questions she led with at her next staff meeting, and she noted a remarkable shift in the conversation and in more positive outcomes. Alisha felt in awe of how much easier and more effective this approach was. And the proof was in the reports. Quality improved in the next quarter!

A year later, after her recommendation, senior leadership, management, many of the nursing staff, and a handful of physicians had gone through a series of AI workshops that literally gave them the ability to turn their culture around simply by changing their conversations. Alisha thought about her conversations with staff these days. They were appreciative and inquiry-based, focusing on what they did well and what mattered to everyone: best and heartfelt care, patient recovery, and a place where everyone thrived.

She also realized that her focus of attention had shifted. Instead of seeing the staff themselves as problems, she was seeing their actions as possibilities. Her conversations with them were very different from those she had had a year ago. These were conversations worth having, and the results they produced were creating positive change throughout the medical center.

For example, the emergency room staff engaged members of clinics and urgent care centers in productive conversations focused on getting people to use the ER only when needed. They mapped their clinical care strengths and specialties across the city. They asked questions to inspire possibilities and new ways of thinking, as well as ways to work together to help prospective patients choose the right location for care. Such questions included, What would have to happen for every citizen to know where to go to get quick and reliable care during the day and after hours? How do we make sure transportation is available to move people where they need to go? The result was a Right-Care, Right-Place plan to help patients learn over time where to go and how to get there. The staffs worked together and developed a system that was delivering right care in the right places. Ultimately, this meant the ER team was serving patients who really needed emergency care. It also meant less chaos and crowding in the ER.

What Alisha and most of the staff discovered was that conversations that were appreciative and inquiry-based fueled productive and meaningful engagement. These conversations were generating exceptional outcomes. The staff throughout most of the medical center had developed a sense of unity and commitment to one another because they intentionally engaged in these kinds of conversations. They routinely thought of innovative ways to improve care and consistently put patients— and one another—at the center of all they did. The results spoke for themselves. The work climate changed significantly. This positive vibe made the medical center a place where people wanted to work. Employee retention improved and staff absenteeism declined. Even when the patient census was high, staff received consistently high ratings that reflected outstanding performance and commitment to excellence.

For Alisha, these positive changes rolled over into her family and personal life just as her frustration had. Alisha found herself initiating more Appreciative Inquiry–based conversations at home, much to the joy of her partner and her children. She found her AI training was every bit as applicable at home and in her community service work as it was at the medical center.

Understanding how appreciation and inquiry enhance relationships as well as productivity and performance is a lesson that Alisha's whole team learned. In our next story about a struggling bank, you will see this point as something that Kamal Amari and Mary Wellington understood well and practiced in their leadership. Kamal and Mary had taken over failing banks and turned them around a number of times. Their success was, in part, due to their capacity for appreciative and inquiry-based conversations. Even when taking over Community One Bank didn't turn out the way they had hoped, great conversations still made all the difference to that bank's employees and customers.

The relationship is the conversation.

Community One Bank stood as a refuge for the small business owner, first-time homebuyer, and teenager opening a first checking account. Located in the outskirts of Detroit, Community One never focused solely on making money. For the original owners, the goal was to provide quality service in a comfortable environment where people served their neighbors and friends. Early on, they had done well, but times had changed. The bank had been struggling financially for some time. One morning the owners gathered the staff to tell them the bank had been sold.

This news came as a shock to the staff. None of them had been privy to the bank's financial problems. Elizabeth Randall had been with the bank for thirty-eight years when the change in ownership occurred. She had long-standing relationships with her customers, who were more than merely deposit and withdrawal statements. For Elizabeth, her customers were like family. In response to the news, she declared sharply, "I'm not going to work for one of those big banks. They don't care about staff or customers. They only care about making profits!"

When the transition occurred, the former owners introduced Kamal and Mary as experienced bankers with a long track record of turning around struggling banks. "I can't promise you this is going to be easy," Kamal told the assembled staff. "I *can* tell you that if we work together and do this as a team, we can save this bank and continue the tradition that Community One has established over the years. I want to be honest with all of you," Kamal continued. "Given the financial issues with the bank, we will be looking at staffing, overtime, and operating policies and procedures. For the bank to survive, we need to cut costs and meet revenue goals on a budget so that we are financially solvent to take care of you *and* our customers. This means that everyone will have to do more with less."

"I knew it," thought Elizabeth. "They're going to destroy everything we've worked so hard to build here." Kamal and Mary met with each employee individually, and when it was Elizabeth's turn, she prepared herself for the worst. However, the meeting was not at all what she expected. There were no closed doors, and no staff were fired. Elizabeth was completely caught off guard at how their meeting started off.

"Thank you so much for coming to talk to us, Elizabeth," welcomed Mary. "Kamal and I are excited to meet with you. We understand that you have the longest history with the bank and that no one knows this place better than you. We're hoping you'll share your best experiences with us about what makes Community One great. We also want to know what gives life to this bank and community?"

Kamal and Mary smiled reassuringly in response to Elizabeth's "deer in the headlights" expression. Elizabeth stammered, "You want to know what makes the bank great? But I thought we were losing money!"

"The bank *is* losing money," said Kamal, "and we *do* need to make changes, but we don't want to change what it is about this bank that customers love. We want to learn about what you and the other team members have done to engender such loyalty on the part of this community. We need your experience and knowledge, Elizabeth, and we hope you'll partner with us to turn the bank around."

"Of course, I will," Elizabeth agreed. She was stunned at the direction of the conversation. For the next hour, Kamal and Mary peppered Elizabeth with questions, such as "What do you love most about your job? What wishes do you have for the bank to best serve its customers?" Elizabeth found herself drawn to the magnetic energy of these strangers. They laughed as she regaled them with stories of funny things that had happened over the years. Between their positive questions and these stories, Elizabeth began to remember why she loved her job. Elizabeth also found herself wanting to work with Kamal and Mary in whatever way she could to help the bank succeed.

Over the next eighteen months, the new management worked alongside the staff to make sure everyone was aware of the bank's financial situation and how the changes they were making affected their viability. Naturally, not all the interactions were problem-free. Some difficult conversations occurred. On one such occasion, Kamal asked Elizabeth and another account manager, Ram, to come to his office.

"Elizabeth and Ram," he began, "come in and have a seat. I have a couple of areas that we need to address together. You know we've been working on time management and new accounts over the last month. Elizabeth, it is still taking you too long to open new accounts, and Ram, you don't open many accounts." Elizabeth and Ram each felt a flush of embarrassment, but it vanished quickly because Kamal continued without blaming. Instead of focusing on what they were doing wrong, he acknowledged their strengths and asked them to team up. "Elizabeth, you open the most accounts every month. Ram, you are faster than anyone else at opening accounts. Would you two be willing to work together to combine your areas of expertise to create a fast and effective process for landing new accounts for the bank?"

This led to a great conversation between Ram and Elizabeth. They pooled their strengths and knowledge to develop a replicable process for opening accounts. Elizabeth learned some effective shortcuts on the computer, and Ram learned ways to engage customers and invite them to explore accounts that would be beneficial for them. When they presented their model to Kamal, he seemed quite impressed with their design. He asked them to introduce other staff members to their plan and bring them up to speed with their new process.

Kamal's leadership style had turned a problem into an opportunity to improve things for everyone at the bank and also to strengthen the leadership capacity of upper-level staff. Elizabeth had come to understand that Kamal and Mary truly had both the employees' and the bank's best interests at heart.

Their appreciative, open, and collaborative style of management had converted Elizabeth from skeptic to cheerleader.

Things at the bank were now going extremely well. The bank was not completely out of the red, but it was getting close. Then the 2008 Great Recession struck. To make matters worse, the city of Detroit and all its surrounding communities were hit hard by problems with the automotive industry, the lifeblood of the local economy. This perfect storm negatively affected the bank, and almost overnight the bank went from "on the road to recovery" to "no longer financially viable."

Kamal and Mary gathered the team and announced that a decision had been made to close the bank permanently. Elizabeth and her coworkers were disappointed but not surprised; they understood the economic crisis. Despite the closing, Kamal and Mary pulled off a near miracle. Instead of a massive backlash because of the closing, the whole staff came together and worked as a unified force to close the bank down quickly and efficiently while taking care of the customers. In the end, what could have been a terrible situation ended up as a success. Every customer was counseled on what was best for them, every account was reassigned somewhere else, and every staff member who wanted a job was provided with assistance and training to ensure that they had an opportunity to find alternate work, even at a competing bank.

These two stories illustrate the power of Appreciative Inquiry to foster the kinds of conversations that result in team and organization excellence. AI conversations are worth having because they enliven people, strengthen relationships, unleash creativity, and move organizations forward fast. They can turn a workplace spiraling into despair into a culture of well-being and innovation. They can pave a pathway to possibility and innovation, even in the face of unforeseen and unfortunate circumstances. Leaders such as Alisha, Kamal, and Mary are skilled at facilitating these kinds of conversations. They know how to draw out the best in people, inspire engagement and commitment, and spark creativity and innovation by using two simple appreciative practices.

Through our combined fifty-plus years of teaching and working with clients using AI, we have learned firsthand the power of asking generative questions and positively framing a situation. AI literally allows people to transform conversations into fuel for productive and meaningful engagement. The material developed in this book reflects our research and practice of AI with our families, organizations, clients, and community groups. Though the names of people and some organizations have been changed, the stories in this book are based on real people. Their experiences provide information that will help you deal with even the most challenging situation by using two simple practices. This book provides the insight and tools to help you engage in conversations worth having.

If you're thinking "Success doesn't come from putting on rose-colored glasses and just having feel-good conversations," we agree. And, we assure you that, no matter how complex the challenges or problems you face at work, at home, or in your community, you can have a great conversation about them. We offer a simple framework for doing so.

## Conversations Worth Having Framework

It begins with understanding the nature of your conversations and how they affect the outcomes you get. In the next chapter, you'll learn that our conversations fall into four categories;

each category influences our relationships and potential. You can foster productive and meaningful outcomes by intentionally choosing to have conversations worth having. One element of our framework supports intentionality, while the other two foster conversations worth having. Figure 1.1 illustrates the cyclic relationship among the three elements. There is no hierarchy to these elements; each is essential for success.

Tuning in allows for self- and other-awareness, giving you the choice to be intentional with your conversation. Asking generative questions and using positive framing fosters conversations worth having.

*Tuning in* is a strategy to support intentionality in your conversations. Unless we tune in to the unconscious influences

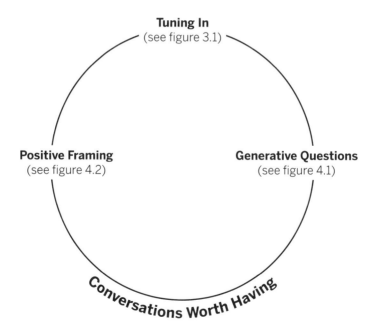

Figure 1.1 Conversations Worth Having Theory of Change

on our perceptions, those aspects of our body-mindset that are beneath the surface of awareness will govern our reactions. Awareness puts you into the driver's seat of your interactions. You might tune in before starting a conversation or before responding to someone who has triggered you. Ultimately, the goal is to develop the skill to stay tuned in during all your conversations, including with yourself, so that you can be the conductor of your life.

Tuning in allows you to choose how you respond in any situation, which makes it easier to use the two AI practices (generative questions and positive framing) in your interactions. Again, the three elements are in relationship to one another without a specified sequence of steps. You might begin by asking generative questions or just as easily begin with a positive frame. You might find yourself tuning in during the middle of a conversation, realizing you (or the other person) are responding defensively. You can shift that dynamic by asking a generative question or reframing the conversation. Regardless of where you begin in the circle (figure 1.1), all of these elements—tuning in, generative questions, and positive framing—are essential for consistently fostering conversations worth having.

As we've said, it's simple and not easy. It requires intention and practice. Is it worth the effort? It is, if you want to increase your capacity to flourish.

Each element of the framework will be explained in the coming chapters. In addition, you will explore the five AI principles that guide successful practice. You will learn how to initiate AI conversations at the organizational level to develop the kind of connections and relationships that foster strategic thinking and high-performing teams. You will come to understand the science behind these practices and learn why holding an attitude of curiosity and consistently seeking to contribute value are your best assets for strengthening your relationships with family, friends, and colleagues—and bringing more of what you want into your life. In the next chapter, we begin with the notion that conversation is the foundation of everything we do and create together. *The nature of our conversations determines our well-being and our capacity to thrive.*

# What Kind of Conversations Are You Having?

> *The moment of questioning is also the moment of choice, which holds the greatest leverage for effective action and positive change.*
> —*Marilee Goldberg*

**Conversation** is a constant in our lives, whether it consists of our internal dialogue or our interactions with people. We all know these conversations affect us, but we may not realize how much influence they have on our well-being and our capacity to thrive. Not sure about that? Have you ever been in a great mood and having a really good day when a short interaction with someone turned the whole thing sour? Or perhaps you were having a lousy day and a simple conversation suddenly brightened your outlook. In their research, Jeff and Laurie Ford, authors of *The Four Conversations*, actually documented that "the type of conversation you have with the people around you has a profound impact on your experiences, relationships, and accomplishments."[1]

Conversations are almost like breathing. Much of the time, we are unaware of the nature of our conversations and their impact on our experience of being in relationship with others and in the world. It usually takes a significant (emotional) experience for us to actually step back and reflect on the nature of those conversations. Recall Elizabeth's passion and commitment to the bank and how she felt that those who bought the bank would destroy it. She made a lot of assumptions about what kind of conversation she was going to have in that first meeting. She was stunned when her assumptions turned out to be the opposite of what happened.

The nature of our conversations is far more important than we know. After she got into university, Ming Li, the daughter of one of our colleagues, told her mother that as a child she loved having conversations with her. "I felt connected with you. You empowered me to think and contribute, and those times always stimulated new ideas for me," she said. "They also made both of us feel hopeful and excited about the future. I remember going to school after an early-morning conversation about innovation and renewable energy. I was so motivated by what might be possible! How I might one day contribute to that change." Now, as a young adult, Ming is initiating those kinds of conversations with her friends and professors while earning a degree in environmental engineering.

So, what is it that creates conversations worth having? Let's find out by looking at the nature of conversations in general. Conversations have two dimensions: (1) appreciative-depreciative and (2) inquiry-based–statement-based, as shown in figure 2.1.

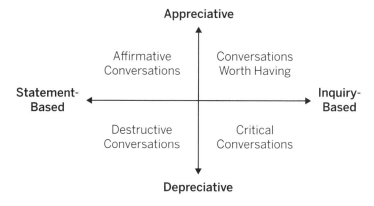

Figure 2.1 The Nature of Conversations

### The Appreciative-Depreciative Dimension

The first dimension describes the nature of our conversations as taking place along a continuum from *appreciative* (adding value) to *depreciative* (devaluing). Adding value to a situation, person, or opportunity can show up in a number of ways. For example, sharing ideas, shedding light on assumptions, augmenting other people's contributions, generating possible solutions, naming important issues, advocating for possible actions, acknowledging other people's contributions, pointing out opportunities, responding to questions with new perspectives, and contributing to planning are all appreciative ways we add value through conversation.

Engaging in such ways deepens understanding, strengthens connections, enhances relationships, expands awareness, broadens and builds human potential, adds new knowledge, or moves us toward desired outcomes.[2] Think about times you've collaborated with others to develop creative solutions to a sticky problem or been publicly acknowledged for great work you've done. Remember how these conversations made you feel? Often conversations like these feel good and are energizing. The value added goes beyond the positive emotions we experience. These conversations literally create an upward spiral of confidence and optimism.[3] They stimulate meaningful engagement and inspire innovative thinking and positive action.

We refer to appreciative conversations as being "above the line" because they elevate our well-being and our access to higher order thinking, creativity, and connection.[4] Figure 2.2 illustrates that above the line we experience positivity, connection, possibility, creativity, and a sense of well-being. We are more open-minded and can access critical thinking; this makes it easier to choose responses that add value. In chapter 7, you will learn more about the science behind this.

The depreciative dimension devalues a situation, person, or opportunity. This shows up in conversations when someone judges or belittles other people's ideas, criticizes others' contributions, advocates for their own ideas without listening to others, continually points out reasons why things will not work, blames others, drives a singular focus, dominates the interactions without making room for others to speak, interrupts or cuts people off, ignores contributions, and complains. Engaging in ways that devalue others is toxic. It actually weakens connection, strains relationships, reinforces assumptions, eclipses human potential, limits possibility, and hinders creativity and movement toward desired outcomes. Think back on times you may have argued with someone or been on the receiving end of criticism. Did you say things you didn't mean or came to regret later? How did those conversations make you feel?

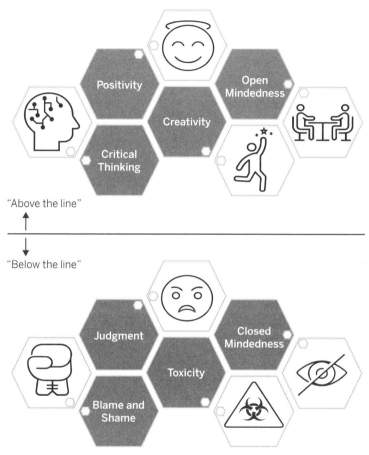

**Appreciative Conversations**

Positivity

Open Mindedness

Creativity

Critical Thinking

"Above the line"

"Below the line"

Judgment

Closed Mindedness

Toxicity

Blame and Shame

**Depreciative Conversations**

**Figure 2.2 Conversations above and below the Line**
Conversations above the line are appreciative, adding value and strengthening relationships. Conversations below the line are depreciative, devaluing people and situations.

Depreciative conversations are often described as exhausting. They can waste time and leave people with low energy, feeling alienated and drained. Research in the field of positive psychology has found that focusing on what is wrong or the negative in an effort to fix something actually narrows our thought repertoire, thereby restricting access to the skills and thinking capacity needed for innovation, critical thinking, and solution-finding.[5] Depreciative conversations can smother creativity, resulting in decreased productivity and disengagement. We refer to depreciative conversations as being "below the line" as they fall into the full range of depreciative interactions. When you're in a conversation, ask yourself, "Where am I: above the line or below?"

## The Inquiry-Based–Statement-Based Dimension

In the second dimension, conversations are either *inquiry-based* or *statement-based*: we are either asking questions or making comments. When we ask questions grounded in genuine curiosity, we typically generate information; reveal hidden assumptions, perspectives, or knowledge; expand awareness; make room for the emergence of possibility or opportunity; deepen understanding; or initiate change. Such questions build relationships, connection, and awareness; they add value and are appreciative in nature. Recall a conversation in which someone's questions resulted in your feeling more connected to them or inspired to take action. What kinds of questions were asked?

On the other hand, questions can arise from a place of judgment, bias, or criticism. Such questions are often rhetorical or pejorative, devaluing people. They are depreciative in nature. Think back to a time when you or someone else asked questions that left you feeling disempowered or critiqued. What kinds of questions were asked in that situation?

Then there are statement-based interactions, made up of declarative statements. These comments can add value (affirmative statements) or can devalue (destructive statements). When statements are appreciative, people may be saying positive things about people or situations or advocating in ways that contribute or point to important facts. Such conversations are valuable and have a positive impact on people and situations. Statements that are depreciative in nature often show up as criticism, blame, and general negativity. The seeds of division are sown, leaving little to no room for learning and growth.

Combining these two dimensions—appreciative versus depreciative and inquiry-based versus statement-based—gives us a way to understand the nature of our conversations and their impact. It suggests there are four basic types of conversations or interactions:

1. Conversations that add value through appreciative questions and dialogue: we call these *Conversations Worth Having*.
2. Conversations that add value through appreciative comments and statements: we call these *Affirmative Conversations*.
3. Conversations that devalue through depreciative questions and defensive interactions: we call these *Critical Conversations*.
4. Conversations that devalue through depreciative comments and statements: we call these *Destructive Conversations*.

At the heart of every conversation there is tone and direction: How is the conversation making us feel, and where is the conversation taking us? Is it moving us above the line or below the line? Many of us find ourselves stuck in conversations that are depreciative in nature. These drag us down and zap energy. Intentionally shifting our conversations to be appreciative and inquiry-based can transform our relationships and workplace outcomes. Think about conversations you've had with family members, friends, colleagues, or your boss. How did you feel after a conversation that you thought was worthwhile? After a critical conversation? A destructive conversation? Or, simply, an affirmative conversation? Which of those conversations had the greatest impact on your sense of well-being or helped you, your colleagues, or your team move forward?

When Kamal asked Elizabeth and Ram to come to his office at the bank to talk about their performance, he could have used several conversational options. The problem was *taking too much time to open accounts* and *not opening enough new accounts*. The tone and direction of the conversation would have been depreciative had he said, "We have a problem. Why is it taking you so long to open accounts? Why do you open so few accounts?" Instead, he stated the problem and reframed it by asking a generative question, inviting his staff to pool their expertise and co-create a new process for opening accounts at the bank:

> *Elizabeth, you open the most accounts every month. Ram, you are faster than anyone else at opening accounts. Would you two be willing to work together to combine your areas of expertise to create a fast and effective process for landing new accounts for the bank?*

It's important to note that he did not ignore the critical issues. He named them, without blame or shame, and focused the conversation on desired outcomes. This created an appreciative tone and a positive direction for their interaction. Such an approach contributed to Elizabeth's and Ram's motivation to learn, grow, and succeed. Their conversation was productive because of that. The result helped them both improve their productivity, while it also supported excellence for all account managers. Tone and direction influence our health, happiness, relationships, actions, and success in life.[6] Our conversations are worthy of our care and attention. Let's take a closer look at each of these four kinds of conversations and how they show up in our lives.

## Conversations Worth Having

Paul put out a text to members of his team on Slack, a cloud-based collaboration application: "Just had a great conversation with @François!" François texted back, "Just took @ paul up on offer to drop by Café Verte and had a fun conversation. He's an interesting guy! I look forward to chatting with him again."

When asked, "What made it a great conversation?" Paul replied, "We were both interested in growing the digital economy in our region, and that's what stimulated our getting together. We didn't know each other, and we were wide open to learning new things. François has an interesting background, and, in asking about one another, I learned he has an unusual perspective on opportunities here. In general, I tend to focus on the differences that people bring rather than the similarities. I like that François doesn't agree with me on everything and knows things that I don't. I asked him what he'd like to see happen at a futures institute,[7] and he came up with some ideas that had never crossed my mind. It got me thinking. When he asked why I asked that question, I shared my dream of creating satellite futures events throughout the region. Then we were off and running about possibilities. It was really worthwhile.

It was stimulating, positive, and full of potential! And I got to know another techie in our community!"

What made it a conversation worth having was its appreciative tone and positive direction; it was *both* appreciative *and* inquiry-based in nature. The men's genuine interest and openness to one another, which created room for each of them to add value to the conversation, made it appreciative. Generative questions were asked about one another's experience and perspectives; this surfaced new ideas and possibilities. The tone was energetic and expansive. The direction spiraled upward as the two men learned about each other and generated possibilities together. Great conversations are generative. They allow for *the creation of new images and metaphors, and they change how people think.*[8] We can recognize conversations worth having by their tone and direction. They are

- Meaningful
- Mutually enlivening and engaging
- Geared to generate information, knowledge, and possibility
- Solution- or outcomes-focused
- Uplifting and energizing
- Generative
- Productive

The appreciative and inquiry-based conversation between Paul and François resulted in a new friendship, the surfacing of diverse perspectives and skills, the generation of ideas and possibilities, and the energy for moving forward.

We've all participated in conversations worth having, which by their nature are appreciative and inquiry-based. They are typically rich and deep. You know you're in a great conversation when you are energized and filled with positivity (positive emotions), images, and actions. Your thinking and creativity broaden and build. Your awareness expands and triggers insight. In the workplace, such conversations fuel productivity, performance, engagement, and satisfaction, all of which promise to support excellence.[9] In communities, new futures are made possible. At home, such conversations create strong family bonds and support the potential of family members to thrive.[10]

Unfortunately, this is not the nature of most of the conversations we have with ourselves,[11] nor is it the nature of most conversations being broadcast in the media. Too often, at home, at work, on social media, in the news, and in TV programming, we engage in or witness critical and destructive conversations. You might think, "Well, that's just human nature." But recall the impact of such conversations on the medical center's ability to thrive. Over time, depreciative conversations destroy our sense of well-being and eclipse our potential to contribute. They negatively affect workplace engagement, team performance, productivity, and organization success. Furthermore, such conversations fray our relationships, deplete our energy, waste time, and depress our will to try, much less excel. Such conversations affect us physically, mentally, and emotionally, draining our potential for well-being.

If it is "just human nature" to focus on the negative or to be critical, some might say we should simply resign ourselves, even though we know that this depletes us across the board. On the other hand, we also know that it is human nature to connect and create. Human nature is adaptable, and habits are flexible; the best response is not resignation but intentionality. We can learn to shift our conversations. Before diving into how to do this, it is valuable to understand the nature of the other three kinds of conversations: affirmative, critical, and destructive.

### Affirmative Conversations

A high school teacher affirms, "Samantha and Tamir, you've done an excellent job on your project! It's clear you both put in a great deal of time, and you met the criteria for earning an A. I would like you to present your project to the class tomorrow."

"Thanks," said Samantha and Tamir in unison. "You helped us a lot; we could never have done such a good job without all your support," added Tamir.

"Well, that's what I'm here for," the teacher replied. "All I did was give some suggestions and leads on where to look for things. You both did all the hard work and put it together in such a polished final product. You should be very proud of your work!"

This is one form of an affirmative conversation. The tone augments positive emotions and good feelings, yet it is non-directional. The impact it has on the emotions can nonetheless inspire forward movement and motivate positive action. Another form of affirmative conversation is mutual advocacy: you share your ideas and others share theirs. Such conversations typically transition into one of the other types of conversations. If debate, criticism, and argument arise, you've moved into a destructive interaction. By contrast, a conversation worth having emerges if people in that conversation seem genuinely curious about one another's points of view or how their ideas might come together. As soon as questions are asked that generate new knowledge or invite understanding, the interaction becomes a conversation worth having. Affirmative conversations center on the following:

- Genuine admiration
- Acknowledgment
- Generative feedback and feedforward[12]
- Motivation/encouragement
- Advocacy

The difference between a conversation worth having and an affirmative conversation is palpable. The latter, like the one Samantha and Tamir had with their teacher, simply feels good. It strengthens relationships, reinforces positive behavior, and encourages excellence. Yet it lacks the vibrancy and dynamic energy of a conversation worth having. Engaging in affirmative conversations is important because they foster a climate that favors potential and creativity. On their own, however, these conversations are not sufficient to generate new knowledge or innovation.

Over time, engaging in affirmative conversations may be experienced simply as "being nice." Without generative questions being asked, affirmative conversations can result in a friendly but superficial environment where no real learning and growth take place. We may like and appreciate one another after such conversations, but we don't achieve the same depth of relationship or find possibilities for the future that develop when we inquire deeply together.

Excessive or insincere affirmative conversations backfire. Inauthentic appreciation can create a toxic environment over time. These interactions may show up as "talking nice" to someone's face while making negative comments behind their back or using affirmation and praise to gain something of value for oneself. Such expressions and manipulations become self-evident to everyone involved, except perhaps the person perpetrating them. Over time, these are experienced as depreciative conversations.

## Critical Conversations

The boss ordered the team into her office, and it was clear she was not happy. Stefan looked down and sighed as his shoulders slumped at the boss's words. "Who the h!@! submitted this to the executive committee?" she asked. "Does this look professional to any of you?" she snapped as she threw the ten-page report across her desk. Stefan had not thought it was ready to send, but she had demanded the report be sent no later than yesterday, and she would not entertain a conversation about a later date. As team lead, Stefan spoke up: "I told you it wasn't ready, but you said to send it anyway."

"Oh, so now it's *my* fault?" she barked.

"I'm not saying it's your fault, I'm just saying I tried to tell you we weren't ready," said Stefan.

"So why *weren't* you ready? Is someone not pulling their load? This isn't the first time your team has missed deadlines. Now the VPs are breathing down my neck, thinking we don't have what it takes to do this job."

"In all fairness," Stefan said, defending himself and his team, "this is an exceptionally qualified team. As usual, we didn't have the time or the equipment to move any faster in getting the results you wanted. We're at the mercy of our equipment and the process. Once we get things set up, all we can do is wait." The rest of the team was silent, staring at their feet and feeling uncomfortable.

The boss dismissed them with a wave of her hand. "Get back to work, and let me know how soon you can get a *professional* report ready for me. This time I want to see it *before* it goes out!"

The tone and direction of this conversation are quite different from those of the previous ones. The boss's depreciative questions drained the energy out of the room. The conversation was a volley between defense and offense, attack and deflection. The interaction eclipsed any sharing of valuable information that might have generated productive solutions. It lowered morale among team members and added another brick to the wall between the boss and her employees. The team left the conversation knowing that they didn't live up to their boss's expectations and yet not quite sure how to move forward. This conversation hindered creative possibilities for delivering on desired outcomes; it was a matter of starting over or waiting for the process to be completed.

We've all been part of such conversations, sometimes as the critic and sometimes as the one critiqued. Oftentimes the critic does not see herself as being critical. In intimate relationships, critical-sounding conversations seem to be part of the territory. For example, a seemingly benign kitchen remark such as "Sweetheart, why don't you use just one pan? It will be so much easier and less work in the end" can launch a cascade of undesired results and friction. The person asking this may say, "I'm just trying to be helpful," but there's an underlying judgment or assessment that can be heard in the tone. It's not a genuine question; it's a suggestion in the guise of a question. The other person, depending on past interactions, assumptions, and current state of mind, can easily feel criticized and may snap back, "Why do I have to do it *your* way?"

Judgment and criticism lie at the core of a critical conversation. The person being asked the question typically experiences a negative emotional response: defensiveness, fear, shame, unworthiness, anger, or disempowerment. Depreciative questions often reflect an unequal power dynamic (boss-subordinate, parent-child, teacher-student, more experience in the kitchen versus less), where the person being asked the question experiences being "one-down." Such deficit-based questions negatively affect the mood and confidence of people.[13] These kinds of interactions typically lead to disengagement and lowered productivity. They also fray the fabric of relationships.

Avoiding critical conversations does not mean we should avoid critical situations, mistakes, problems, or inappropriate behavior. It's a matter of how we address those issues. If we can address the issue itself, without judgment or assumptions, we're more likely to foster a conversation above the line. Conversations about critical issues are vital to the success of individuals, teams, and organizations; however, when held as critical conversations, they often fail to create positive change.[14] Arguments between couples can bring issues out in the open that need to be aired, but how those issues are raised and discussed makes all the difference.

Strong relationships reinforced predominantly by appreciative conversations can easily survive a critical conversation. Research shows that the best results for teams and relationships stem from a 6:1 relationship (six positive interactions to one negative).[15] Over time, if critical conversations dominate the conversational landscape, they eventually weaken relationships, limit potential, and eclipse generativity. In effect, they start to become destructive conversations. When the ratio falls below 3:1, things begin to fall apart.[16]

## Destructive Conversations

Shane and Jean-Luc were standing around the coffee machine. "If I have to listen to Claudia talk about her sales goals one more time, I'm gonna hit something," said Shane in exasperation.

"I know what you mean," added Jean-Luc. "She's so oblivious to how she makes the rest of us feel."

"Yeah, well, she didn't get all those sales on her own. I'll bet the manager steers some of them her way. You've seen how they look at each other, haven't you?" Shane insinuated.

"Whoa, I didn't know that! That's not fair," fumed Jean-Luc. "That annoys me. To think I have to put together a proposal with her tomorrow! I will have to be careful with her and keep my cards close to my chest. She'll probably make me do all the work, and then she'll take all the credit."

You can see where this conversation is going and also how it will influence Jean-Luc's ability to work with Claudia the next day. This is a destructive conversation with no chance of a positive outcome. It creates or reinforces differential power dynamics, generates a negative tone, and creates roadblocks for progress toward desired outcomes. The conversation is full of statements that devalue Claudia, her work, and the manager. Without her even being present, the relationship between Claudia and her two colleagues has been fractured. Jean-Luc has been set up to anticipate a negative interaction in which he loses. Unless Jean-Luc realizes the destructive nature of his conversation with Shane, his interaction with Claudia the next day is likely to be critical or destructive. There is little chance they will have a highly productive and meaningful engagement.

For those in an intimate relationship, a critical or passive-aggressive question such as "Why do you always have to leave your stuff lying around?" can trigger a destructive conversation between partners: "You are such a nag!" "I wouldn't have to nag if you'd put your stuff away!" "It's my house, too, and I like my stuff where it is! You are such a control freak!" "I'm not trying to control; I just like a house that's clean and neat. It's better feng shui; energy gets caught up in clutter." "Oh jeez, now it's feng shui!"

This couple is talking past one another—full of judgment and criticism. By not listening to each other, they deny one another's value in the process. The conversation is loaded with blame, name-calling, and fault-finding, which then trigger attack-and-defend stances. Not only are such conversations *not* worth having, they are toxic. They destroy both relationships and the potential for excellence. When such conversations are the norm, they are actually predictive of low-performance teams and even divorce.[17]

You can tell you are in a destructive conversation because it drains life and energy from those involved. It spirals downward, augmenting negative feelings and images. People on the receiving end do not feel valued and do not contribute value. No one feels good about the dynamic. Once defensiveness is triggered, statements become reactionary, fueled by negative emotions that tear down ideas and narrow both creativity and critical thinking. Relationships grow more and more strained, and over time trust erodes. Just as they did at the medical center, such conversations create a toxic environment. Such a climate results in lower productivity, disengagement, dissatisfaction, and loss of connection. If the situation continues, relationships disintegrate. Organization teams fail to perform well. Employees mentally check out, quit, or form cliques that generate divisiveness. Families can even fall apart. These destructive conversations often take the form of any of the following:

- General deficit-based narrative: blaming, disempowering, claiming authority, or otherwise minimizing the worth of others
- Arguing or debating, without listening to one another
- Bullying
- Trash-talking about other people
- Commanding and controlling
- Advocating strictly for oneself, with no inquiry into what others are thinking

The tone of destructive conversations feels bad and stimulates negative emotions. The direction often sits in spin cycle, going nowhere. Instead, the negative tone amplifies.

Take a few minutes and think about times you have been engaged in each of the four types of conversations in your personal and professional life. What was the tone and direction of the conversation? Those are two key indicators of the kind of conversation you are having and whether you are above the line or below. The goal is to engage with others above the line—in appreciative conversations. Your success in staying above the line is correlated with your ability to choose to be intentional with your words.

For most of us, this is a challenge. We often speak without awareness of where we are, what we are doing with our words, and how our conversations are influencing others. This is especially true when we're stressed, defensive, burned out, or fearful. In the next chapter, we'll share a strategy to support mindfulness. Tuning in will help you shift your body-mindset in ways that prime you for a conversation worth having.

# 3

# Who's Driving? Tune In

Knowing yourself is the beginning of all wisdom.
—Aristotle

**In our work** with clients and colleagues, we discovered that an important element was missing from our first edition. It became apparent that conversation is like the water in which fish swim, so omnipresent that we lose awareness that it is the medium in which we navigate our lives. Our conversations are fateful. What we think, say, and do influences every moment in our lives. When we converse without self-awareness, our conversations are channeled through our resting body-mindset. In other words, our current frame of mind, our dominant thoughts and feelings, and our current physical state drive the conversation.

Our resting body-mindset lies beneath the surface of present awareness. This means we are at the mercy of subconscious drivers such as judgment, assumptions, biases, and low blood sugar. To consciously step into the driver's seat requires self-awareness and choice. It entails tuning in to what's going on to make the subconscious conscious. With awareness, we can choose our words. We can decide how to respond, what to say and ask. In other words, we can intentionally foster conversations above the line. This chapter offers a technique for doing that.

First, let's see how the resting body-mindset influences Jake's and Timmy's interactions. Jake hadn't slept well in weeks, hadn't touched his bottle of water all day, and had inhaled his lunch while working to meet looming deadlines. At 3:00 p.m., Sandy stuck her head in his office, smiled cheerfully, and asked, "Do you have those stats for me yet?" He snapped back at her with such fierceness, it took her breath away. She disappeared quickly. Jake sat stunned at the way he'd just treated his colleague, unleashing a cascade of self-loathing, blame, and shame. He left that day sure his colleague would tell others what a terrible team member he was. He was angered by that thought and felt she'd be right. Jake was having a most depreciative conversation with himself. He was definitely below the line.

Timmy said something embarrassing in front of his whole class, and all the kids had laughed at him. Even his teacher had smiled before moving on. He ran home after school. On his way to his room, his mom reminded him, "We have family photos in an hour. Please be ready." "I'm not going," he shouted as he slammed the door. His mom, who'd had a very long day at work, stormed after him, opened the door, and was ready to scold him until she saw his face. She stopped and took a deep breath. She felt her body relax and her demeanor soften. Then she asked with genuine concern, "What's going on?" Timmy's initial comeback to his mom's reminder ignited what might have been a depreciative conversation. However, his mom recognized immediately he was below the line, and she intentionally shifted gears to the conversation worth having in that moment.

The difference between Jake and Timmy's mom was that she'd tuned in to both Timmy and herself. Pausing and taking a deep breath gave her the space to intentionally change the trajectory of their interaction. Her ability to become aware of her body-mindset and her son's was the difference between initiating a depreciative conversation and initiating one worth having.

## Unseen Influences beneath the Surface

Our resting body-mindset is influenced by our past, present, and anticipated future. Our worldview, beliefs, assumptions, and biases have been formed as a result of past conversations and experiences. We begin taking in messages about how to make sense of the world the moment we are born. Cultural frameworks, norms, and biases mix with our interpretations of our experiences and the way we make meaning with others. These slip beneath the surface of awareness and influence our perceptions and subsequently our conversations. Our emotions and nervous system are influenced by the amount of sleep we get, the food we ingest, and the amounts of oxygen we take in and water we drink. And if that's not enough going on beneath the surface, our nervous system is also influenced by other people's state of being.[1] If you've ever felt calm and content and then suddenly found yourself agitated moments after someone walked into the room—or the opposite, been anxious only to gain a sense of peace when another person entered—you've experienced this influence.

Like the iceberg that sank the *Titanic,* what lies beneath our surface often sinks our relationships and efforts (figure 3.1). When we are not aware that all these factors are influ-

*Until you make the unconscious conscious, it will direct your life and you will call it fate.*
*— C.G. Jung*

encing our conversations, they drive the interactions and often drive them below the line into the depreciative realm—just as they did for Jake and Timmy.

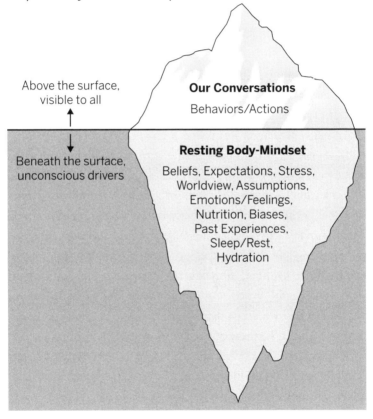

**Figure 3.1 Tip of Conversations**
Unseen factors influence our conversations. When you are aware of them, you are better able to foster conversations above the line.

Jake was clearly stressed about work at the outset. On top of that, he hadn't slept well, he was dehydrated, and it was midafternoon. He likely wanted to meet the needs of his teammates and worked hard to do good work on time. This was the perfect storm for a below-the-line conversation. Timmy very likely experienced an immediate threat response to being laughed at in school. Our need to belong is one of the strongest drives we have; it can be more important than food or shelter for some. Timmy was clearly below the line and set to collide with his mom's stressed body-mindset. This could have driven a below-the-line conversation if they'd both remained unaware. Fortunately for Timmy, his mother tuned in to his inner state and then her own.

### Location, Location, Location

When our conversations are below the line (depreciative), they generate stress, negative emotions and actions, and disconnection (refer to figure 2.2). Similarly, when our body-mindset is below the line (we're experiencing stress, negative emotions, and disconnection), we tend to foster depreciative conversations. If we don't tune in and become aware, we can end up in a downward spiral that tears at the fabric of relationships and inhibits our capacity for well-being and success. Recall Alisha's experience from chapter 1. Month after month, she spiraled below the line.

Conversely, when our conversations are above the line (appreciative), they generate connection, creativity, productivity, learning, and engagement. And when our body-mindset is above the line (we're feeling connected, creative, and engaged), we tend to foster appreciative conversations. One key to intentionally fostering conversations worth having is to know where you are: above the line or below the line.

Due to all the factors discussed above, in each moment of our lives, our resting body-mindset is primed for either above-the-line or below-the-line conversations. When we are below the line, we are primed to be defensive, closed, and committed to being right. This is the location of the fixed mindset.[2] It is where we are driven by fear and scarcity as well as being dehydrated, undernourished, and tired. Here, life can feel overwhelming, hopeless, and unmanageable. We typically feel the need to protect ourselves to survive. Jake and Timmy were below the line, experiencing blame, shame, and negative projections (on themselves and others).

When we are above the line, it is easier for us to connect with others, to feel empathy and relate. Above the line, things seem possible in life; creative solutions emerge because we are curious and open. We often shift from "me" to "we" in the focus of our interactions, which makes it easier to listen to other points of view, broadening our perspective. Above the line, we naturally have appreciative conversations.[3]

Where are you in this moment? Are you above the line, open and curious about whether this idea applies to you? Or are you below the line, closed and dismissive? How do you know where you are? We'd like to offer you a simple strategy to increase your understanding of where you are. We encourage you to tune in.

## Tune In

Locating yourself means tuning in to your body-mindset. The technique we use to tune in is this: *pause, breathe,* and *get curious.* Pausing stops the current momentum. Breathing deeply stimulates the parasympathetic nervous system, calming your stress response. To maximize the relaxation response, take a deep breath and hold it briefly. Then, exhale slowly, longer than your inhale. Then take another breath. This gives you a moment to expand your awareness, to observe yourself in the moment. Doing just this has the potential to move you from protect to connect. Why? According to Andrew Huberman, "The reason a breath practice is so powerful is that it's a bridge between our unconscious, reflexive states and our conscious, deliberate state."[4]

---

**Try This Exercise from Huberman**

"When you inhale, realize that you are literally taking control of your brain and mind; and when you exhale, allow that ability to take hold in positive ways. Intentional breathing reminds us that we are in control of our inner state at the most fundamental level. And you can grab ahold of that sense of control anytime stress hits or when you simply want to appreciate a moment and be more present."[5]

---

After breathing, get curious. This further increases your awareness, allowing you to consciously choose to be in the driver's seat: "Where am I? Where are others? What's the bigger picture or context?" Such questions challenge our thinking and invite us to choose positive intention.

In this space between stimulus and response lies our opportunity to choose.[6] What kind of conversation do I want to foster? What needs to happen in this moment to support that? It's also an opportunity to explore what lies beneath the surface, influencing our present reaction:

- What's this conversation really about?
- What assumptions am I making?

- What beliefs and preconceived ideas are influencing my perception?
- What else might explain what's happening?
- Am I hungry? Thirsty? Tired? Hot or cold?
- What emotions am I experiencing, and what are they telling me?
- What don't I know that might be important in this moment?
- What's driving the other person's behavior and actions?
- What do I want to have happen; what's my agenda?

Here's a simple example that may sound familiar. Becky has a habit of sharing her opinion without being asked, especially with her husband. After attending a Conversation Bootcamp,[7] she realized her comments were often unconsciously driven and damaging to the person she loved. She was determined to start tuning in before offering her opinion.

Her first success in doing this came one morning while she and her husband were walking their dog. Her husband was sharing a story about advice he'd given someone he was mentoring. She felt her critic wake up, but instead of telling him why that advice was wrong, she paused and took a deep breath, giving her a moment to get curious. It took no more than a few seconds for her to ask herself, "How is my opinion relevant?" She thought, "He's sharing a story about something that's already happened. My opinion is irrelevant and off topic. What would deepen my understanding of the story?" Then she asked out loud, "Why did you give him that advice?" His response surprised her. With this added information, his advice seemed spot on. (Imagine that!)

Tuning in gives us the opportunity to choose to intentionally foster a conversation worth having instead of unconsciously reacting from beneath the surface. When we are tuned in and stay tuned in to the world within and around us, we are in the driver's seat of our conversations. This supports our ability to intentionally foster and maintain conversations worth having, even if they become confrontational. Our ability to listen deeply while engaging in conversation is an important aspect of tuning in and staying tuned in.

### Listening: The Silent Partner in Conversations Worth Having

Tuning in requires us to listen deeply to our inner state and to others. Asking who's in the driver's seat applies to listening as well as speaking. When we just listen without an intention to listen deeply, what we hear is filtered and scripted by those drivers beneath our radar (figure 3.1). This means we are at risk of listening with a closed mind, a closed heart, and a closed will. Our preconceived ideas, beliefs, and motivations may have us listening to find fault, judge, negate the other, or defend our point of view. This works well in a debate, but not if we want to have a conversation worth having.

Being intentional about listening takes practice. It means listening with an open mind, willing to entertain another's ideas; listening with an open heart, willing to empathize with another person's experience and understand a situation from his or her point of view; and listening with an openness to new possibilities and new ways of going forward. The Chinese symbol for the verb "to listen" captures the essence of what it means to listen deeply. The complex character is a combination of the characters for eyes, ears, heart, and undivided attention (see figure 3.2).

In preparation for listening deeply, you can do a quick one-minute emotional audit: "What am I thinking? What am I feeling? What do I want to happen now? What am I going to do next?" Then choose to be present: pause, take a deep breath, center yourself, relax, and invite just a little more _____ (e.g., space, openness, light, compassion, curiosity, interest).

When we are aware and able to choose to foster conversations worth having, listening deeply comes more naturally. Our questions are authentic. We are genuinely curious about the other person, interested in learning and understanding that person's ideas and experiences, so we listen with an open mind and heart. We are interested in finding ways to achieve optimal outcomes, so we listen willing to entertain new ideas and possibilities. Engaging in such conversations comes down to our capacity to be intentional, to be in the driver's seat.

## Coming out of the Tunnel

When we are not in the driver's seat, it's like driving in a tunnel. We can't see, hear, or understand anything beyond our

Figure 3.2 The Chinese Character for "to Listen"

biases, mindset, beliefs, and needs, which reflexively steer and sometimes recklessly drive the interaction. When we choose to step into the driver's seat with awareness, we emerge from the tunnel. The horizon opens up. We see ourselves in relation to others and to the situation. We discover opportunities to see from another's point of view, expand our world of possibilities, and find shared pathways forward. From this vantage point we can effectively use two simple practices to foster conversations worth having: generative questions and positive framing. In the next chapter, you'll learn about these practices and how others are using them to intentionally strengthen their relationships, improve well-being, and generate success in their organizations.

# 4

# Two Simple
# Appreciative Practices

*Creating a positive future begins in human conversation. The simplest and most powerful investment any member of a community or an organization can make is to begin with other people as though the answers mattered.*

*—William Greider*

**We saw** in chapter 1 how Alisha changed the tone and direction of her conversations at the medical center simply by asking questions that challenged her ordinary ways of thinking and changed her frame of reference. This altered everything. She got curious about her role in the current outcomes. She reflected on the focus of her conversation and what she really wanted to talk about. These kinds of questions shifted her frame from focusing on data to focusing on actual patient outcomes. It expanded her thinking from *employees as problems* to *employee ideas and actions as possibilities*. From this new frame of reference, a different set of questions emerged, inspiring solutions and more effective interactions than previous critical conversations. These questions helped her staff focus on what was working and sparked ideas about what else might work. The answers enabled them to replicate success and create new possibilities.

Likewise, Kamal and Mary at the bank intentionally framed their first meeting with Elizabeth to set the stage for an appreciative tone and positive direction. Inviting her to share her best experiences about what gives life to the bank and the community resulted in a conversation worth having.

The two Appreciative Inquiry (AI) practices Alisha, Kamal, and Mary applied were generative questions and positive framing. It can be difficult to separate these practices in action because they weave together to create conversations worth having. Nonetheless, they are in fact distinct. It is worth understanding how each is practiced and contributes to productive and meaningful interactions. Each practice can alter the tone and direction of any conversation. You can begin with generative questions, which naturally create a positive frame because you are inquiring into what adds value. You can even ask a generative question in the midst of a negative interaction to turn that conversation around. Or you can start with a positive frame.

### Generative Questions

The practice of asking generative questions invites you to adopt an attitude of curiosity. When we are genuinely curious, we naturally ask generative questions. Our colleague Gervase Bushe best describes generativity as "the creation of new images, metaphors, or physical representations that have two qualities: they change how people think so that new options for decisions and actions become available to them, and they stimulate compelling images people act on."[1] As a result, generative questions have the following outcomes:

- They might challenge our ordinary ways of thinking and doing: "What else might explain what happened?"
- They may make room for diverse and different perspectives: "How do you see it?"
- They can surface new information and knowledge: "How did they manage this process at your previous plant?"
- They often stimulate creativity and innovation: "What might be possible if we merge marketing and development?"

When dealing with any issue, even a difficult one, generative questions result in conversations that create trust, positive energy, and the transformative power to move the relationship or system forward in a positive direction. Generative questions focus on what adds value, the best of what is, and what might be. The result: breadth of understanding, new ways for solving complex problems, and compelling images for collective action.

Our work with clients has deepened our appreciation for the need to clarify how generative questions change our thinking and how they differ from problem-solving questions. Most of us are good at problem-solving, and we've been rewarded for coming up with solutions. Problem-solving is valuable when trying to solve mechanical problems, and it doesn't work well for human systems or complex challenges. If we don't tune in, this mindset primes us to ask questions that are really solution focused. For example, the front-of-house manager of a restaurant and a waitstaff member are arguing about a procedure. The general manager overhears them and asks, "What if you try _____?" Her question is really a solution, and coming from the general manager, it may end the conversation.

Sometimes this is expedient; however, it eclipses the potential for the parties to understand their different perspectives and discover their own solution.

We've also learned from our clients that we often ask ourselves questions when we don't know what someone else is thinking or feeling. Anytime you find yourself asking yourself about other people, don't answer! In the workplace, managers and leadership teams routinely do this: "How might we motivate the team to be more productive? What kind of training should we provide?" Such questions encourage us to make stuff up, to guess. This can be costly, and it's unnecessary. The people with the answers are right there. Ask them. Turn these into generative questions: "When you are engaged and enjoying your work, what motivates you? What kind of training will help you be more successful on the job and in your professional life?"

We find that generative questions tend toward divergence. They broaden our focus of awareness, thus changing the way we think and see. These questions encourage us to take in more of what is around, within, and beyond us. They can invite us to step back from our ordinary ways of thinking and doing, creating space for us to become more conscious in any given situation. This includes becoming aware of our assumptions, biases, body-mindset, actions, and choices. It also means seeing and understanding the broader context: your own and other people's perspectives, assumptions, ways of knowing, data and information unknown to us, positive deviance,[2] and the larger context that includes the purpose of the conversation. These questions typically result in two outcomes: making the invisible visible and creating shared understanding.

For example, in the restaurant scenario above, the general manager might have asked, "What's going on? How is this impacting each of you? What's important for each of you in resolving this? What's important for our customers here?" Once all the invisible information is shared, a solution may be apparent. On the other hand, it may be valuable to continue asking generative questions that invite people to think and see beyond their ordinary ways of seeing and doing. These generative questions make room for emergence. Such questions inspire possibility, disrupt ordinary ways of thinking and doing, and make room for creativity and innovation. These questions typically result in two outcomes: they generate new knowledge and inspire possibility.

Continuing with our restaurant scenario, any member of this group might ask, "What ideas do you have that would be win-win-win? How do other restaurants handle this? What if the customer was the solution?"

Let's look at a couple of examples illustrating how asking generative questions shifts our thinking and seeing. Bob was busy working on his responsibilities for a department project. Mia walked into his office and he fretted: "I'll never finish on time." Mia asked how he was doing the work. After he explained, she asked, "How did you decide to do it that way?" He paused for a moment and suddenly realized he hadn't decided; he'd just done it the way he'd always done it. In that moment his thinking changed. He realized there might be a better or easier way; in fact, the team never challenged any of their thinking before they dove into doing the project. Mia had asked a question that made an invisible assumption visible. Once visible, it could be challenged, and it exposed a greater opportunity. Following this interaction with Mia, Bob called the project team together to clarify their purpose and the customer's why, making more of the invisible visible and creating a shared understanding around desired outcomes.

They then began asking generative questions that invited greater creativity for the "how." These questions invited innovative thinking. Bob and Mia asked the team questions such as "How might we rearrange or redesign our process to eliminate steps and time? How might we rethink our siloed effort and develop a more systems-level approach for the project? And, if we were starting from scratch with no preconceived ideas about how to accomplish this project, what questions would we ask, whom would we involve, and how might we do it?"

*Innovative solutions can be found in what is already working.*

Generative questions are just as valuable in solving complex global issues, as was the case for Jerry Sternin. In the 1990s, Jerry worked for Save the Children, an international nongovernmental organization working on behalf of children's well-being. The government of Vietnam asked Save the Children to help it with childhood malnutrition in the south of the country.[3] Jerry landed in Vietnam and was promptly told by the foreign minister that not everyone was pleased he was there and that he had only six months to make a difference. Any ideas about doing traditional problem-solving, such as achieving clean water, setting up educational programs on nutrition and sanitation, and eliminating poverty, were clearly not going to work. Jerry challenged his ordinary ways of thinking about childhood nutrition by asking himself a generative question: "I wonder if there are families where the children are thriving?"

This question inspired Jerry to bring together teams of mothers from rural communities to help him answer it. He asked them to weigh and measure all the children, in hopes of finding some children that were not malnourished. Meanwhile, he talked with as many people in the community as he could to discover their eating norms. Generally, mothers did the food preparation, families ate twice a day, and children ate with adults and fed themselves. The children ate soft, clean food (no crustaceans), and if they were sick, they did not eat; however, he found inconsistencies. The data the mothers gathered showed that there were, in fact, small pockets that represented exceptions to the norm in the community: there were children of very poor families who were healthier and bigger than the standard. His generative question made the invisible visible.

Jerry asked another generative question: "Is there something the mothers of these children are doing that is making the difference?" Observation and conversations with these mothers surfaced important differences; they did not follow the cultural norms. In these families, children ate the same amount of food, but it was spread out over four meals. If the children did not eat on their own, their mothers fed them. These children were served small shrimp and crabs as well as sweet-potato greens, which were considered a low-class food. In addition, when children were sick, they ate. The difference in diet was significant: these children were receiving more protein and vitamins on a daily basis. Jerry's research teams had discovered a native solution to the problem of malnourishment. As a result, Save the Children implemented a program for mothers with healthier children to teach other mothers in their community how to feed their children in a more beneficial way. In six months, they made a positive difference in the well-being of these families—and discovered a solution that could be replicated.

Jerry had challenged ordinary ways of thinking about the problem. Instead of asking questions about fixing the structural and cultural issues related to malnutrition, he looked for positive deviance. The solutions were already present in the community. He discovered them by asking generative questions.

### Shifting Depreciative Conversations with Generative Questions

Sometimes we find ourselves in the midst of a critical or destructive conversation because no one is paying attention to the nature of the conversation. Shifting a depreciative conversation to an appreciative one can be initiated by using generative questions. In the following story, you will see how Gabriela asks a simple question that changes the tone and direction of a conversation.

Gabriela, an organization development consultant, attended a reception on the last evening of an AI workshop. She was talking with the provost of a large midwestern university about a new project it was undertaking that promised to engage students and improve student learning outcomes. The provost was complaining, "We have invested so much time and money in this powerful new learning management system, and I just can't get the faculty on board. It's so frustrating, especially for students. I sometimes wonder whether they simply don't get how beneficial this is."

*Inquiry and change are not separate moments.*

Gabriela had been listening and commiserating. She had her viewpoint about academicians, which lined up with what he was saying. She added to this depreciative conversation by asking, "That's pretty typical of faculty, isn't it?" and "Why are they always so resistant to anything new?" Suddenly, she realized that she was asking depreciative questions, which was keeping this critical conversation going. She thought, "Okay, let's give this AI approach a test drive. We'll see if I can change this conversation just by asking a simple question to flip the focus."

The next time the provost paused, she asked, "Are there any faculty who are on board with what you are trying to do?" Before she even completed the sentence, the provost brightened, stood taller, smiled, and with enthusiasm and a completely different tone declared, "Oh, yes, the College of Management is completely on board! They've adopted this wholeheartedly!" Then he went on to describe all the things the faculty were doing and the successes their students were having. But Gabriela wasn't listening anymore. She was in awe of how easy it had been to shift the conversation.

Generative questions work just as well in families as they do in organizations. Monica was able to change the conversational dynamic with her son by asking such a question. She had been in the midst of a recurring argument with her teenage son, Aiden. She was tired of the same old interaction that never produced a way forward. Aiden wanted to borrow the car over the weekend to go "do things" with his friends, and Monica didn't like the idea of his joyriding, with the possibility of getting into trouble. Their critical conversations had created a rift between them, which saddened Monica, but she didn't know what else to do.

Suddenly, in midconversation, it occurred to her she could use the practice she'd learned at work for shifting the tone and direction of a conversation. When Aiden started to reiterate the argument, Monica held up her hand, paused, took a deep breath, and said, "I really do understand why you want the car, and I hope you understand why I'm worried for your safety and well-being. So, how can we have a more productive conversation? How can we come to some agreement that allows you to get the car and me to feel comfortable that you'll make good decisions, even if your friends are pressuring you?"

Aiden was stopped in his tracks. This time it was his turn to pause, and then they began a brand-new conversation that promised to be worthwhile—and it was. Monica's questions allowed Aiden to let his mom know that he did understand. He shared that sometimes he was glad he hadn't been allowed to have the car because of where his friends ended up. But other times, he had missed out on experiences he wanted to have. At those times, he felt she was being overprotective. On hearing that, she realized she hadn't even considered that part of the stalemate might be her own refusal to let go. Monica and Aiden eventually arrived at an agreement to start small and keep expanding car privileges as trust and confidence grew between them.

Monica shifted the conversation out of critical debate and into a conversation worth having by asking a generative question that reframed the focus of the conversation. This simple action shifted the tone and direction of the conversation. It allowed both of them to step back, reflect for a moment, be more open and honest, and hear one another. That shifted the outcome of their interaction. This is one of the most valuable practices you can develop for building strong relationships, expanding the potential of a group, surfacing possibilities in the face of challenges, and rapidly moving toward desired goals.

All Monica did was ask a generative question that shifted the focus of the conversation to a desirable outcome, one they both wanted. When Monica asked her son to help create a solution that would work for both of them, Aiden stopped advocating for himself and opened up to his mother's needs as well. All Gabriela did was ask a generative question about the positive opposite of what the provost was saying. Their questions flipped their conversations *in the moment*.[4] This is one of the simplest tactics for shifting a conversation from depreciative to appreciative.

These stories are only a few of the many client stories we have gathered that demonstrate the power of asking generative questions. Such questions shift our thinking, make room for innovation, and invite people to show up, engage, and participate. When people are invited to share their knowledge and ideas, it encourages everyone to stay open and listen. This broadens and builds our access to critical thinking and creativity.[5] Such questioning expands possibilities for action, increases the odds for new knowledge and innovative solutions, and paves a path for flourishing.

### What Question Do I Ask?

Asking generative questions starts with curiosity and an open mind. We suggest this begins with tuning in and reflecting on your own frame. Where is your focus of attention? Are you open to any answer, or is there an agenda or a set of assumptions behind your question? Recall Alisha before she brought AI into the medical center. Declining statistics were her focus of attention. *People must not be doing their jobs* was her assumption. She had a negative frame. Her questions arose from that frame. They were depreciative in nature, leading to critical conversations. By tuning in and challenging her focus of attention, she opened up to possibilities that great care was already being given to those patients who were satisfied. From that new perspective, she automatically found herself asking different questions. She became curious about what was already working and how the staff might replicate those behaviors. Her change in focus of attention ignited generative questions.

Begin by asking yourself, "What is of value and what will add value? Do we need to strengthen connection or understanding? Am I missing anything? Do we have all the information to move forward? Do we know where we're going? Are we ready to be creative?" Figure 4.1 provides a quick reference for the four primary categories for generative questions.

Here are a few examples of generative questions in each area:

- *Make the invisible visible:* What don't we know? What else might explain a person's action or behaviors, besides what I am currently assuming? What hidden assumptions, beliefs, rules, or norms might be influencing our thinking? How might diverse expectations be influencing

**Figure 4.1 Awareness and Outcomes from Generative Questions**

what's possible? What is the experience that another is having, and how is it important in this moment? What's the bigger context for this; how is it relevant? What's taking up time and money? What exactly do we want to accomplish here?

- *Create shared understanding:* What information or perspectives do others have that might add value? How do others understand or experience the situation? What is their story? How is this relevant to the work we are each doing? What future are we hoping for? How are individuals or departments going to be affected? What outcomes are desired? What does the client or customer actually want? What is essential and what might we let go of?

- *Generate new knowledge:* How might current ways of thinking or configuring resources be getting in the way of innovation? What happens if _____? How might we combine your ideas with their data? How are all these data points linked; what's the simplest explanation? How might the customer design this? How is the customer going to use this? How might we organize if we were starting from nothing? Where can we find people who are doing this well, and what can we learn from them?

- *Inspire possibilities:* How might we create pathways forward that work for all? What have others done? Where is this already working well, and what can we learn from that? How might we _____? What if _____? How might we improve on the best of what is? What could we do if money and time were unlimited? How might we do this if we had to have a process in one hour?

Table 4.1 provides more examples of generative questions.

Before introducing the second practice, we need to remind you that generative questions may not always seem positive in and of themselves; however, they always add value and have a positive effect on people and situations. This is especially true if someone needs to feel seen, heard, and valued before moving forward—someone like Colleen.

Colleen left the meeting spitting mad—again. She'd been ignored during the meeting, her idea wasn't considered until a guy repeated it, and she'd been routinely interrupted whenever she tried to contribute. Trevor, her administrative assistant, overheard the guys leaving the meeting talking about her in pretty negative terms. He knocked and went into her office. "Are you okay?" he asked. "No," she muttered. "I'm really tired of the way I'm treated by the other leaders. I am so tired of being disrespected by men around here." Trevor asked for the details of her story to deepen his understanding and to make sure she was heard. Her response sounded like he'd invited a depreciative conversation. She was frustrated as she retold her experience with the other senior leaders, emphasizing that this happened every time they got together. Trevor listened and affirmed her feelings.

Just being heard began to shift Colleen's energy. Trevor could hear the shift in her sigh and resignation: "I'm done fighting to be a valued member of the team. I just may have to resign." Trevor asked, "Do you know if other women have this same experience here?" Again, this may sound like a depreciative question because it's asking about the problem, but such a question broadens awareness. Trevor's questions made the *invisible visible* and created *shared understanding*. They began to identify some important cultural issues that needed to be addressed. That adds value. When Colleen replied, "There

**Table 4.1 Examples of Generative Questions**

| What Your Question Can Do | Examples |
|---|---|
| Elicit information, stories, ideas, and perspectives | *Alisha's question to the staff: When are patients satisfied?* |
| Tap experience | *You've done something like this before. What was your experience? What worked well for you?* |
| Allow strengths to show up | *How might each of you contribute to the success of this venture?* |
| Surface best practices and elements of success | *What best practices in the industry are you familiar with?* |
| Move toward solutions or to information and data that inform possible solutions | *Jerry's wonderment: What are mothers of healthier children doing?* |
| Identify new ways of thinking, new possibilities, opportunities, and aspirations | *As you think about thriving digital communities, what do they have that we need if we are to develop a thriving digital economy?* |
| Inform what you might do, the results you might want | *Monica's question: What can we do that allows you the car and me my sense of peace?* |
| Make room for new knowledge, creativity, and innovation | *Forget completely about how we have done this in the past. If you were designing it today, what would you do?* |
| Deepen connections | *How do you see it? What's important to you about this project?* |
| Strengthen relationships | *Can you say more about what you mean when you say there's no opportunity for you here? What are possible opportunities you are seeking?* |
| Engage those on the sidelines | *What do you think, Elizabeth?* |
| Generate understanding | *Can you say more about what you are thinking? Help me understand your perspective.* |

may be; I'm not unique." Trevor asked, "What if there's an opportunity here to create positive change for every woman who may be experiencing this?" This shifted the conversation. Colleen hadn't thought about her problem as an organization issue. She perked up as the focus shifted from her personal experience to this being a cultural problem that needed to be addressed. The two of them had many more conversations after that, all focused on creating a more equitable and inclusive workplace. Colleen went on to inspire culture transformation throughout the organization over the course of the next two years. Trevor's generative questions definitely fostered a conversation worth having.

### Positive Framing

Remember when Kamal called Elizabeth and Ram into his office? He wanted to talk with them about how long it was taking to open accounts and how few were actually being opened, respectively. He could have used a critical tone and direction with each of them. Instead, he framed the conversation around working together to create a model for *rapid new-account generation*. This was the desired outcome. It made it easy to invite Elizabeth and Ram to help figure out how to do that. Kamal brought a positive frame to that conversation. Positive framing is not specifically focusing on the positive, but it does result in positive outcomes.[6] It is about focusing attention and action on where we want to go or on what it is we want more of. More often than not, it is highly beneficial to ask generative questions that expand awareness before creating a positive frame, which will then guide a conversation about change or forward momentum.

A positive frame opens the door for conversations that move us toward what everyone in the conversation wants.

Such framing draws people in and inspires curiosity, imagination, and interest about moving toward a shared and desired outcome. For examples of positive framing, see table 4.2.

You can apply positive framing in virtually any situation, conversation, evaluation process, feedback session, meeting agenda, planning process, interview, or interaction. You can do this at the outset of a conversation, or you can shift a conversation if you realize it's depreciative. If you started your conversation with generative questions that made the invisible visible and created shared understanding, you might be ready to shift the focus of the conversation to desired outcomes, which is a positive frame. No matter what the situation or with whom you are talking, you can frame (or reframe) the focus in a way that inspires a conversation worth having. The dynamics of our conversations are always influenced by our focus of attention (frame) and by the questions we ask. Mark's story illustrates this effect.

Our framing and questions are fateful.

Mark, a midlevel manager in a Fortune 100 company, was preparing for a tough conversation with an employee who was very good at her job. There was one major problem: she was routinely late for their weekly meeting and sometimes missed deadlines. He and his mentor were talking about how he might frame this conversation. Mark was smiling as he mused, "Before you taught me the two basic AI practices, I would have seen Melissa as the problem. I probably would have said something like, 'We have a problem; you are always late and miss deadlines. You have to change.' I would have framed a critical or possibly a destructive

**Table 4.2 How Positive Framing Draws People In and Inspires Engagement**

| A Positive Frame . . . | Inspires Curiosity, Imagination, and Engagement |
|---|---|
| Our employees feel valued, and each of them collaborates with a highly productive team. | • *I want to work there! What company is this?*<br>• *How do you know employees feel valued?*<br>• *What contributes to feeling valued?*<br>• *What makes them productive?*<br>• *How can we do more of what you do so our employees have the same experience?*<br>• *Imagine what it would be like if that were the case here!* |
| Employees look forward to their quarterly performance reviews. | • *Really? Why? What goes on in your reviews that makes employees like them?*<br>• *What would have to happen for my employees to look forward to these conversations?* |
| Let's plan our vacation so each of us feels like it was our best vacation yet! | • *That sounds awesome. I want to spend lots of time in the water!*<br>• *Does it matter what kind of water? Because I'd love to go to the beach.*<br>• *How does everyone feel about seeing a few shows?* |
| Our students thrive, regardless of whose class they are in. | • *How is that possible?*<br>• *What do you mean by "thrive"?*<br>• *What do you do to help them thrive?*<br>• *How do you get all teachers and students on board?*<br>• *How can we spread this to all our schools?*<br>• *I want my children enrolled in your school!* |
| In our town, we're talking across all sorts of divides: racial, gender, and political. And we're finding ways we can all live together well. | • *How did you do that?*<br>• *How did you get people to the table?*<br>• *What do you talk about?*<br>• *We're trying to do that but we keep bumping up against fear and resentment. How did you get beyond that?*<br>• *Who helped lead this?* |
| Imagine that after five years we could say that we've made great strides in reducing our environmental footprint each year. | • *I'm up for that!*<br>• *Where shall we start?*<br>• *My department has already been trying to do this. I can share what we've been doing.*<br>• *We may need to make some policy changes. Anyone interested in focusing on those?*<br>• *How do we get people engaged and committed?*<br>• *What can the city/management do to set a high standard?*<br>• *How are we going to measure success?*<br>• *I wonder what other cities/organizations have done?* |

conversation and asked critical questions. I know exactly how that would have played out!"

His mentor nodded and asked, "So, how *are* you going to frame your conversation with Melissa?"

Mark replied, "Well, I'm still not totally sure, which is why I wanted to talk with you. Here's what I'm thinking about doing: Instead of making her the problem, I'm thinking about focusing on a high-performance team and framing the conversation around behaviors that affect the team and our performance. I thought I would start by saying, 'You do exceptionally good work, and your input is very important to our team's success. Because of that, it's really vital that everyone arrive on time, if not a few minutes early, to our meetings and also to make deadlines on time. When you're late, it affects all of us. What ideas do you have for how we plan and schedule things that could resolve this?' What do you think?"

Mark's mentor smiled and said, "That sounds like a productive frame. I'm wondering if there are some things you don't know, perhaps some assumptions you or the team might be making." This generative question gave Mark pause. After taking a deep breath and getting curious, he responded, "You're right. I don't know why she might be late; she's actually usually on time." Mark's mentor encouraged him to begin with questions to increase his awareness and then transition to his frame if it still fit. As he left Mark's office, he added, "Remember to think about your role as well."

It's important to note that Mark was not going to skirt the problem; rather, he was planning to address it head-on and invite Melissa to be part of the solution, just as Kamal did with Elizabeth and Ram. The practice of asking generative questions and using positive framing has allowed Mark to maintain good relational dynamics with his employees while resolving issues that are negatively affecting overall team performance. The result is a department that has a strong sense of well-being and a team that is flourishing. In this particular situation, beginning with generative questions will help make the invisible visible for both of them. Melissa may still feel bad because the problem is the result of her actions, but the focus is not on her; it is on clarifying the situation and on moving toward a desired outcome. This allows her to share potential issues that may be impeding her ability to be on time, and new information that arises has the potential to surface solutions.

Positive framing is about intentionally shaping a conversation that invites engagement and produces positive outcomes. This applies at work, at school, at home, in our community outreach, and even when we have internal conversations with ourselves. We always recommend that you begin where you are when you start practicing positive framing. If you're like we once were and most of our clients, you'll start with a problem-oriented or negative focus of attention. When this is the case, simply reframe the focus. A process for reframing a conversation, task, or topic can begin with a technique we call *flipping*.[7] It's a simple way to reframe the depreciative to the appreciative.

### Flipping

After his mentor left, Mark spent time thinking about his mentor's reminder about assumptions and his role in contributing to the problem. He had not considered that he himself might somehow be playing a role in Melissa's being late and had missed the obvious question, "What was making her late?" Just asking himself those generative questions shifted his thinking. Recognizing he was missing information and considering that he might need to own some responsibility made him feel more open and less critical of her. He thought through the flipping process so as to shift his original depreciative frame to an appreciative one. He took the time to get very clear on the impact Melissa's tardiness was having and what the outcome of her being on time would be for the department. His mental process went something like this:

- *What is the problem?* Melissa is routinely late and misses deadlines.
- *What is the positive opposite of the problem?* Melissa is routinely on time and meets deadlines.
- *What is the positive frame?* (What would be the impact if Melissa were on time? What is the desired outcome?) The team has a strong sense of cohesion: performance improves, while trust, mutual respect, and collaboration are solid. All these help us sustain *excellence.*

Notice that the steps to reframe, moving from problem to positive frame, are stimulated by generative questions, especially the move from positive opposite to the new frame. These questions generate both a new perspective and a broader context for the conversation. The new frame typically inspires curiosity. For Mark, reframing helped him put the issue in a broader context for why it was important for team members to be on time. It allowed him to begin with a focus for the conversation that he was sure Melissa wanted also and one where he could point at all the positive ways she was already contributing.

It also made him wonder if there were other things that could be done to build cohesion and how he could better contribute to that. Were there things he might have done differently to set the stage for success? By not doing them, had he set Melissa up for failure? That consideration influenced his state of mind and openness when Melissa arrived for their one-on-one meeting. Mark started the conversation by saying, "Melissa, I want to ensure that we have a strong team grounded in trust, responsiveness, mutual respect, and cohesion because I think it will allow us to be remarkably successful together. What do you think?" Melissa replied with some hesitation, as she wasn't sure where this was going, "I agree; I hope I am contributing to that."

Mark responded, "I hope I'm doing all I can to contribute to that as well, but I'm not so sure I am. I'm glad you and I are on the same page with this. You do excellent work, and your input is very important to our team. You certainly are contributing to our success. I am noticing something that may interfere with this, and I'm curious about it because it's not like you. I'm sensing some frustration among team members during our Wednesday early morning meetings. When you're not there or when something isn't turned in on time, it means they can't move forward because you have important information to share. Is there something about Wednesday morning that is problematic?"

Melissa felt embarrassed, but it seemed that Mark was open to her input. So she shared, "The meetings I'm late for are scheduled at 8:00 a.m. on Wednesdays, and I have a very difficult time getting here on time on that day. That's the only day I drop my son, Connor, at day care. All other days, my husband takes him, but he can't on Wednesdays. If we could schedule our standing meeting for 8:30 or 9:00 a.m., or for any other day, I can assure you I'll be on time."

Mark looked shocked, then asked, "Is that *all* it will take? Surely, we can find another time. We'll reschedule at our next meeting." He realized he'd never asked people about the timing of the meeting.

"And, about deadlines," added Melissa, "I hate it when I miss deadlines too; that's not the kind of reputation I want to be known for. I'll admit sometimes I'm just late, and I need to work on being timely. However, there are times when members of the team set deadlines without understanding what it will take to meet those deadlines. I should probably speak up when I know it's not likely I can meet that deadline, but I feel like I'll be letting the team down if I don't try."

Recognizing that his leadership played a role in this dynamic, Mark responded, "I want you to know that each of us owns a piece of the responsibility here. I need to take some ownership for not involving employees in decisions about meetings, and the team needs to make sure that whenever deadlines are set, everyone affected by those deadlines will be in on the conversation. I will take responsibility for addressing this at our next meeting. For your part, Melissa, in the future, please speak up if you think that a deadline is unrealistic, even if it's been set and if you were not present at the time. Doing that actually makes you a better team player. Either we can change the deadline or the team can help brainstorm how they might support you in meeting that deadline. Will that work for you?"

You can readily see that Mark's positive framing and his genuine question at the outset turned a potentially critical conversation into a productive and meaningful one. It helped him shift his body-mindset, priming him to connect. It also grounded the overall conversation in an outcome that both he and Melissa wanted. You can also see the power of beginning with generative questions that make the invisible visible. Melissa's answer to his question took the conversation in a different direction than he had initially anticipated. His openness transformed the conversation. To practice this yourself, use our simple three-step *flipping* process. This is shown in figure 4.2.

> Step 1. *Name it:* What is the problem, complaint, challenge, or the thing you don't want?
> Step 2. *Flip it:* What is the positive opposite?
> Step 3. *Frame it:* What is the positive impact if the flip were to be true? What is the desired outcome that everyone in the conversation wants?

A note of caution when it comes to creating a positive frame. We often approach a problem with preconceived ideas about a solution or with personal biases (remember the iceberg). Here we run the risk of diving into *our* positive frame with very little awareness. George's situation is a prime example.

George was frustrated that his daughter had dropped out of school, wasn't looking for work, and was holed up in her

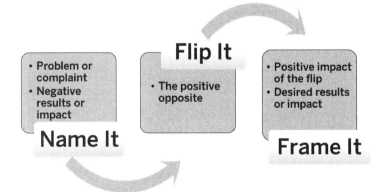

Figure 4.2  Flipping: Framing a Conversation Worth Having

room. He believed college was important if she was going to be successful in life. He also suspected that if she got out and looked for a job, she'd realized she needed to return to college. He brought these unconscious beliefs into his efforts to create a positive frame. He was proud of himself for using the flip, but his conversation was definitely not worth having. It ended as a critical conversation with him once again asking questions like "How far in life do you think you'll get without a degree?" What went wrong? Here was George's flip:

*Name it:* Alexa dropped out of school.
*Flip it:* Alexa is back in school.
*Frame it:* Alexa recognizes that her future depends upon going to college.

George started with an intention to persuade Alexa to return to college; he had an agenda that was driven by his beliefs. As you might imagine, this positive frame backfired.

When reframing a conversation, it's important to have an open mind and to create a frame that will inspire everyone involved in the conversation. This often begins by tuning in and asking yourself, "Where am I?" Tuning in and asking generative questions helps you clarify the real issue. If you already have a specific solution or idea for an action, like George, you limit your ability to create a more inviting frame.

George didn't give up. During their argument, Alexa had asked him a question that made him realize he hadn't really created a positive frame. Just before storming out of the room she asked, "Do you honestly care about my happiness, Dad, or just your idea of what happiness is? You don't even know why I dropped out!" George realized he'd been trying to persuade Alexa with his frame instead of engaging her in a meaningful conversation. Her question inspired him to tune in. Left in the room by himself, he took a deep breath and got curious about his assumptions and beliefs. He realized he didn't really know his daughter—what she wanted or what brought her happiness. He was missing a lot of information and decided he needed to start their conversation with generative questions (to make the invisible visible and create shared understanding). He also wanted Alexa to understand that he'd taken her question to heart, and he wanted to frame the overall interaction around an outcome he hoped she would want as well. He tried the flip again:

- *Name it:* I don't know what matters to Alexa or what makes her happy.
- *Flip it:* I do know what matters to Alexa and what makes her happy.
- *Frame it:* Alexa and I are developing a much stronger relationship, and I know how to support her.

This time he began the conversation by saying, "Alexa, I apologize for our last conversation. What is most important to me is to develop a strong relationship with you and to know how I can best support you." He then began to ask generative questions that arose out of genuine curiosity: "When are you most happy, what are you doing and who are you with? Tell me about a time when you were at your best; what did you value most about yourself and others at that time?" As she answered these questions, he watched her come alive for the first time in a long time. He began to see the intelligent and competent young woman she was becoming. He realized what made life meaningful for her was entirely different from what he wanted for her or what made his life meaningful. The more they talked, the more clearly she (and her dad) understood why she'd dropped out and what her next options might be. There had been a significant shift for both of them. So much so, the next morning, for the first time since she'd arrived home, she joined the family for breakfast and announced she was going to look for work.

When you create a positive frame, check back and make sure the conversation you will be inspiring actually addresses the original issue. Sometimes we get excited about a frame and begin the conversation only to discover that, though it's a conversation worth having, it's not really resolving the issue that needs to be addressed. Once you've created a frame, reflect on it to make sure that it will resolve or dissolve the original issue. For example, Melissa's tardiness dissolves as a problem when she and her boss discover that the real issue is scheduling, and her late work is resolved in their agreement that in the future she will speak up about deadlines. In George's first frame, Alexa was not going to recognize she needed to return to college; the frame was not going to solve what he originally thought was the problem. In George's second try, the original issue was resolved, and a lot of other positive outcomes occurred as well.

Clients have told us creating a positive frame can be challenging. In response, we offer a program called Monday Kickstarters in which people share an issue and then everyone on the call practices creating a positive frame and crafting generative questions. We cover two to three issues per session, and these are recorded and transcribed into blog posts on our website (conversationsworthhaving.today). There you can read many more examples of using flipping to create a positive frame and generative questions to foster these conversations.

Positive framing is helping thousands of people optimally set the tone and direction of their conversations and redirect the focus of any depreciative interaction they encounter. This simple practice lays the groundwork for better relationships and a more effective work environment. It is important to point out that while you can reframe any conversation, it takes willingness on the part of all those involved to participate. Most of the time, people are delighted to focus on what they want. However, if you are engaged in a destructive relationship, one where the other is intent on staying in a destructive or critical conversation, the only option may be to leave that conversation or where possible add others to the conversation. Find a trusted colleague or friend to have an appreciative, inquiry-based conversation about how you can take needed action either to keep yourself safe or to effectively mitigate the negative dynamic.

As we mentioned at the outset, generative questions and positive framing are woven together in an appreciative and inquiry-based interaction. As you begin playing with these two practices, ask yourself: Am I open and curious? Does what I am about to say or ask add value? Am I fueling productive and meaningful engagement? Am I initiating an appreciative tone and positive direction?

Our questions and framing are fateful. They influence our conversations. And those conversations affect both our well-being and our potential to thrive. Conversations fueled by positivity and generativity ignite individual and collective energy. They broaden and build our capacity to innovate and act together with others for desired outcomes. Try asking generative questions and using positive framing wherever you can.

Pay attention to the outcomes. You will see that these two practices facilitate effective and efficient change for you and others in your family, organization, and communities.

In the next chapter, we'll share five rules that will help you tune in more deeply so you can use these two practices most effectively. As we will show, the five AI principles helped Daniel, Ravi, and several other clients expand their ability to engage in conversations that were definitely worth having.

# 5

# What's Fueling Your Conversations?

*Each person's life is lived as a series of conversations.*

*—Deborah Tannen*

**Tone and direction** are simple cues that tell us what kind of conversation we are in. How we got into that kind of a conversation is a different story, yet it is an important one to understand if we want to make sure we have conversations that feel good (on balance) and that take us where we want to go. In chapter 3, we talked about *tuning in* to increase awareness of who's driving our conversations. This makes it easier to be more intentional in our interactions. The Appreciative Inquiry principles, identified by David Cooperrider, provide an added set of guidelines. These principles form a foundation for understanding the dynamics at work in our conversations at a fundamental level. Regardless of the nature of our conversations, these principles govern their outcomes. Tuning in puts us in the driver's seat, and the principles help us reach our destination.

During Alisha's AI training, she was introduced to the five AI principles.[1] Upon understanding the principles, she realized how her conversations with staff about low patient satisfaction continued to reinforce the problem. That awareness changed everything for her. It was essential to her success in applying the two practices. As they did for Alisha, the principles will strengthen your capacity for engaging in conversations worth having.

The five AI principles are as follows:

1. *Constructionist Principle:* Understanding, interpersonal dynamics, meaning, and ultimately our social reality are created through language and in conversation.

    → What we believe to be true is informed by and evolves through conversation.

2. *Simultaneity Principle:* Change happens the moment a question is asked or a statement is made.

    → As words are spoken, our mind, body, and emotions react in a split second.

3. *Poetic Principle:* Every person, organization, or situation can be seen and understood from many perspectives.

    → There is no one truth about any person, situation, or organization; truth depends on perception and focus of attention.

4. *Anticipatory Principle:* The images and thoughts we hold influence our intention and conversation.

→ We move in the direction of the images and thoughts we hold. Our expectations inform what we look for, what we see, and what we hear.

5. *Positive Principle:* The more positive and generative the question, the more positive and long-lasting the outcome.

→ Our questions inspire images, and imagery compels action.

The five AI principles are simple rules that govern our conversations.[2] Understanding how these principles work together helps us stay tuned in and makes us better drivers of productive and meaningful engagement. Here's how:

- If the way we talk together influences understanding, interpersonal dynamics, teams, departments, and organizations (Constructionist Principle), then it makes sense to hold our beliefs lightly and to ask questions, making room for both new knowledge and new meaning.
- If our perceptions and experience change instantaneously in response to how we use or interpret words and actions (Simultaneity Principle), then it makes sense to stay open and ask questions.
- If our focus of attention influences our beliefs and the stories we make up about people and situations (Poetic Principle), then it makes sense to talk about and pay attention to what's working, what's best, and what's possible.

- If our expectations influence what we see, hear, and do (Anticipatory Principle), then it makes sense to stay open, anticipate the best from others, and expect to be pleasantly surprised.
- If our words and the questions we ask have tone and direction that engender imagery that compels us to act (Positive Principle), then it makes sense to ask the most generative and inspiring questions we can and stimulate positive images of what we want more of.

When Alisha learned about these principles, she reflected back on her previous interactions with medical center staff. By focusing attention on what was going wrong (Poetic Principle), she ended up asking depreciative questions that fostered a negative dynamic. Tuning in, she realized she was below the line, driven by the belief that it was her responsibility to make sure quarterly reports improved, but she couldn't do that because the staff were not doing their jobs. She was anticipating she might lose her job because the staff would continue to just make excuses instead of doing their jobs better (Anticipatory Principle). Since she was coming from below the line with depreciative comments and questions, the staff responded accordingly (Simultaneity Principle). It was a downward spiral following the principles to a tee.

She now understood that her critical questions flowed from her thoughts and feelings. Tuning in, she realized that her fear of failure made her look for someone to blame. Those conversations left everyone feeling bad. On top of that, the conversations weren't producing the results she needed. Patient satisfaction and employee engagement kept slipping. Understanding the AI principles made it easier for her to tune in and get curious, challenging her thinking and how she was seeing things. This awareness gave her the power to choose a frame that made way for a more worthwhile conversation. Alisha's entire approach shifted once she realized that the predictive nature of the principles would support success. She also more deeply understood the importance of tuning in to be aware of her frame of mind, assumptions, expectations, and degree of openness because all of these influenced her words. Those words were integral to both the context and the outcome of her conversations.

At her training, Alisha learned that the heart of AI consists of the *cooperative search for the best in people, their organizations, and the world around them* and that solving tough problems from that perspective results in creative solutions, which is *life-giving* for people.[3] When she returned to work after the training, she thought carefully about her approach and her relationships with the people with whom she interacted. In this reflective mindset, she knew the staff cared about patients as much as she did. And, of course, they wanted the medical center to be a great place to work. She still had to talk with them about the poor quarterly reports for their unit. However, this time she intended to have a conversation that was productive as well as meaningful.

Following the Constructionist Principle and the Poetic Principle, Alisha framed her conversation by acknowledging and affirming the staff: "I know we are understaffed and that each of you is working extra hard to make sure patients are well cared for. I have no doubt you want your diligent work and care to be reflected in our reports as much as I do." This created an appreciative context, influencing expectations (the Anticipatory Principle). Then, following the Positive Principle, she asked a generative question that stimulated a conversation worth having: "Let's forget about the reports for a minute. Tell me, where do you feel you are excelling in each of these areas on your floor?"

At first, the staff seemed stunned at the turnabout in the tone and direction of Alisha's question. They couldn't believe that she was setting aside the reports. After a moment of awkward silence, though, the staff began sharing stories of patients who'd been fully satisfied, even to the point of sending thank-you notes and flowers to staff after they had left. Alisha asked them to be more specific about what was unique about those patients' experiences. The ensuing conversation surfaced positive actions that could be replicated.

This reflected the Simultaneity Principle and the Positive Principle in action. Some staff had never even thought of a few of the ideas. Alisha felt delighted with the increased energy and enthusiasm the staff seemed to have for one another and the patients. It was a great conversation and the beginning of the turnaround in performance and ratings. This micro-moment created a macro-movement for positive change at the medical center.

The easiest way to move in a positive direction while uplifting and energizing people is to initiate conversations worth having. To do this, you need to understand and pay attention to what is fundamentally governing your interactions. The idea is to use the principles as a guide to create a context for the conversation that predicts a conversation worth having: what is your shared understanding, what are you anticipating, focusing on, looking to bring about? Let's explore more deeply how the AI principles can help you create great conversations. Each of the stories we share starts with a core principle, yet all the principles are at work in every conversation. These principles invite us to learn how we can drive our conversations in a positive direction in all aspects of our lives.

The first principle, the Constructionist Principle, is foundational to all the rest.

## The Way We Know Is Fateful

*Constructionist Principle: Understanding, interpersonal dynamics, meaning, and ultimately social reality are created through language and conversation.*[4]

At the end of the first month of school, Jamal's favorite class was social studies, and his favorite teacher was Ms. Wittit. He had turned in every assignment, volunteered for extra credit, and even stayed after class to help tutor one of the other kids, who was struggling. He was thriving. While in the teacher's lounge one day, Ms. Wittit shared how excited she was to have Jamal in her classroom and bragged about what a great student he was and how much he contributed to his classmates. Ms. Summers, who had Jamal in her English class, was dumbfounded. She wondered if there could be two Jamals in the seventh grade. She shrugged her shoulders and concluded that he must not like English.

*Our beliefs and perceptions influence our conversations.*

Others might come to the same conclusion, and they would be wrong. Jamal's participation and performance stemmed from classroom interactions, not his subject preference. The frame or mindset the teachers held influenced their understanding of Jamal, what they believed would support his learning, and ultimately the way they engaged with him. Let's take a look at the unexamined framing that these teachers brought to their classroom and the influence that framing had on Jamal.

Ms. Summers grew up in a strict household. Her mom was a nurse, and her dad was in the military. She was raised to believe that success came from disciplined action and attention to what was important. If you had a problem, you dealt with it promptly. Sometimes this meant asking for help, but doing it yourself showed character. Her mother was loving and nurturing. Her dad rarely praised her for good work because that was expected: you work hard, you do your duty, and maybe there is time for play. She believed she could best help students learn by ensuring that they stayed focused on the class material and did good work. This was her frame in working with all her students.

Ms. Wittit grew up in a very different kind of household. Her mother was a naturopathic physician, and her dad was a successful sculptor. Their home was full of laughter, encouragement, and creativity. She was raised to believe that when you were most engaged and passionate about something, you would be successful. If you had problems, you stepped back to see the bigger picture and sought other people's perspectives and support. Her mom was loving and nurtured her strengths. Her dad inspired her to see the world through the eyes of an artist, always looking for possibilities and unique perspectives. Ms. Wittit believed she could best help students by encouraging their passion and engagement with the material and reinforcing their strengths. This was her frame in working with students.

Both teachers wanted the best for Jamal, yet their way of understanding his behavior, based on their personal frames, made a remarkable difference in how they interacted with him. In English class, Ms. Summers was trying to be helpful, though Jamal felt constantly criticized. When he tried to connect with others by making a joke, Ms. Summers admonished him immediately. He often gazed out the window to help him concentrate. Ms. Summers assumed that he was distracted, so she would stand between him and the window, hoping that would help him pay attention. Jamal's assignments were erratic. When they were done poorly or off topic, she asked, in a critical tone, "Why did you turn in such poor work when you are clearly capable of better work?" Jamal would look at his feet and shrug his shoulders. He didn't like English class much.

Ms. Wittit's interactions with Jamal were remarkably different. She believed humor could help students learn, and she saw Jamal's clowning around as a way for him to break tension, make a point, and connect with the other students. Left alone, he was careful to be appropriate and stop himself most of the time. If she needed to redirect, she was careful not to single him out or embarrass him. She noticed Jamal gazed out the window a lot, and she wondered if he might be a highly auditory learner. She knew that auditory learners often look away to concentrate. She tested her theory by occasionally asking him a question about what she'd been saying. He'd turn toward her and answer correctly and promptly each time. Clearly, he was paying attention, so she ignored his window-gazing behavior.

The first time he did poorly on a homework assignment, she stopped him after class and said, "Jamal, you are an excellent student. Your first three papers were spot on and written well. What you turned in yesterday doesn't really reflect the assignment. Is there a reason you didn't write on topic?" Jamal told her that he wasn't really sure what she'd said when she assigned it and was too embarrassed to ask. None of his friends were in this class, and he didn't have anyone to ask, so he'd guessed.

She exclaimed, "Oh my, we have to change that! If you don't understand what the assignment is, imagine how many others might not understand it either. I really need you to make sure I'm clear. What could you say or do to let me know I need to repeat something more clearly the next time?" Jamal thought for a moment and joked, "I could scratch my head and make a silly face?" He demonstrated, and they both laughed. He agreed he'd try that the next time he didn't quite get the assignment. After that, Jamal never hesitated to use the signal for her to repeat something he thought was important. He was making straight As, and he loved social studies. Table 5.1 provides a summary comparison of the principles, working from two different frames.

This is the Constructionist Principle in action. In any given moment, each of us brings to it a wealth of knowledge and experience, plus our personal frame and a set of beliefs that shape and influence our perception. All of these elements influence how we respond to the present moment. First, we "construct" understanding about the way the world works. Then those mental models govern our perceptions, understanding, and subsequent actions. Ms. Summers and Ms. Wittit each developed a unique worldview as they grew up having conversations with their family, friends, teachers, and other influential people. Their worldview governed how they understood Jamal and the meaning they made of his actions. This influenced their interactions with him. Unless we stop, reflect, and become aware that our hidden frame is driving our conversation, we end up reinforcing our own frame and possibly eclipsing others. This simple awareness means that we have the option to choose to be open, challenge our own perceptions, ask generative questions, and entertain a *new* frame.

**Table 5.1 Principles at Work in Jamal's Story**

### Constructionist Principle Influences Belief

**Ms. Summers**
Worldview: A meaningful and successful life comes from following rules, using disciplined action, and solving problems quickly. Therefore, talk about and follow rules, enforce discipline promptly, and problem-solve in order to be successful.

**Ms. Wittit**
Worldview: A meaningful and successful life comes from following your passions and heart, acting from strengths, and using creative thinking to inspire possibility. Therefore, talk about and inspire passion, discover strengths, and make room for creative potential.

### Poetic Principle Influences Attention

**Ms. Summers**
She sees Jamal as a potentially bright student who has some behavior issues that get in the way of his success. She thinks about how to curtail his weaknesses to create a successful learning environment.

**Ms. Wittit**
She sees Jamal as bright with acute hearing and wonders if his shyness may be getting in the way of his success. She thinks about how to leverage his strengths to create a successful learning environment.

### Anticipatory Principle Influences Intention

**Ms. Summers**
If she can spot his behavioral problems when they show up and quickly stop them, Jamal might be more successful. She expects there will be behavioral issues, and she is on the lookout for them. Jamal is afraid to answer her questions because he expects further criticism, which he's heard before: "Well, don't be so silly. Speak up and ask me!"

**Ms. Wittit**
If she looks for ways to engage him and help him use his strengths, he'll be more successful. She anticipates he has strengths and interests, and she's looking for them. Jamal has been supported and encouraged in the classroom, so he expects the same thing when she asks about the assignment.

(continued)

Table 5.1 Continued

| Simultaneity Principle Influences Action |
|---|
| **Ms. Summers**<br>The moment Jamal starts clowning, she quickly stops it so he can learn. Jamal feels shamed and shuts down in response to her public reprimands and her criticism of the assignment. He is afraid to answer her questions. |
| **Ms. Wittit**<br>The moment Jamal gazes out the window, she asks a question to assess his attention. Jamal feels seen and encouraged in response to her questions in class, and he is encouraged to be honest with her in response to what he sees as genuine curiosity about his assignment. |

| Positive Principle Influences Outcome |
|---|
| **Ms. Summers**<br>The questions that are asked are critical in nature, designed to help him improve. |
| **Ms. Wittit**<br>The questions that are asked are appreciative in nature, designed to surface information and encourage Jamal. |

## Change Happens the Moment You Ask the Question

*Simultaneity Principle: Change happens the moment a question is asked or a statement is made.*

Recall in the last chapter how Gabriela suddenly tuned in, becoming aware of the tone and direction of the conversation she was having with the provost. That awareness allowed her to check her negative actions and ask a generative question. Gabriela felt in awe of how quickly the provost's behavior changed and how fast the conversation flipped. In that instant, she understood the power of the Simultaneity Principle: inquiry and change are *not* separate moments.

Her story illustrates how easy it can be to turn a conversation around with a simple generative question. It shows that *change begins the moment you ask a question or make a comment.* To experience this yourself, think of the last time you made a mistake in front of your boss or colleagues or were chastised publicly. Stop reading for a moment and bring the memory in and feel the experience in your body. How does reliving that experience affect you physically, emotionally, and mentally? Now, recall the last time you were praised publicly or were acknowledged at work for excellence. Stop for a moment again and bring that memory in. How does reliving that affect you physically, emotionally, and mentally?

How fast did your state change? You probably found that it was simultaneous with the suggestion. That is the Simultaneity Principle in action. Inquiry and change, for all intents and purposes, are simultaneous events in a conversation. Gabriela's question to the provost shifted his body, tone, and direction instantaneously. She also discovered there were (at least) two stories about the faculty and the project. In one story, faculty are resistant to technology. In the other, faculty are embracing it. Which story turns up in a conversation depends on the frame you are using and the questions you ask (the Poetic Principle). Next, we'll see how Daniel learns the power of the Poetic Principle in his work with First Nations gang members.

## The Story in Front of Us Influences Our Expectations

*Poetic Principle: Every person, organization, or situation can be seen and understood from many perspectives.*

Daniel worked with First Nations youth and had an especially challenging job of trying to help gang members choose a different path. He had been taking these troubled groups on ropes course adventures to teach them teamwork and leadership skills,[5] though without much success. Daniel did not believe these gang members knew much about teamwork or leadership, as evidenced both by their failure to complete challenges and by the life choices they were making. He had hoped that if he could teach them these skills, they might take a leadership role in their own lives.

> Everything we say and do moves us and those around us.

One day a grant came through for him to purchase a portable challenge course, which included training. During his training, he was introduced to a different kind of facilitation: appreciative facilitation.[6] Instead of pointing out why teams failed at activities, this process invited participants to identify moments of success and build on strengths. During the training, Daniel was introduced to the AI principles, and he had a major aha moment, just like Alisha. He reflected on the assumptions and stories he believed about the gang members and understood how those things were influencing the way he saw the teens, what he listened for, and what he said to them. Without knowing it, he had been reinforcing his beliefs in their incompetence, and he felt dismayed that his debriefing style had actually reinforced their negative behaviors.

When he started facilitating with generative questions, a whole different story began to emerge. One of his first questions was simple: "Even though you didn't complete the challenge, what was working for you?" As the teens struggled with this shift in focus, Daniel tried to remember witnessing something that was working so that he could cue them. "Remember when you were able to stay on the beams and began to move the team across the swamp? What did you do to help you stay on the beam and move as a team?" One young man volunteered, "We were holding on to each other. That helped us balance." Then more of them voiced ideas: "We moved slowly, and we didn't pull someone until they were ready." "Sammy wasn't on yet, and he could tell us what was happening because he could see everybody. That helped me focus."

In that moment, Daniel realized these kids actually *had* teamwork and leadership skills. They used them to be a tight gang. He just hadn't looked for them. Over time, his questions surfaced skills in each young man, and some of them discovered they were strong leaders. He now saw his job as helping them realize how capable they were and cultivating their strengths to be effective leaders in the community. Over the next year, Daniel's struggle turned into joy as he watched the potential of these kids emerge. He inspired them to create new challenge activities using the modular equipment, and he taught them appreciative facilitation so that they could teach younger boys what they had learned.

Daniel experienced the Poetic Principle. When he was watching for failures, he saw failure. When he was looking for teamwork and leadership, he saw leadership and team competence. It was neither magical nor Pollyannaish. It was simply a matter of choosing a positive perspective and then asking generative questions.[7] The next story builds on this principle, as Ravi discovers that creating a positive frame for a conversation and asking a generative question are not enough to ensure that you'll have a conversation worth having.

## Expectations Influence Conversations and Possibilities

*Anticipatory Principle: We move in the direction of the images and thoughts we hold.*

On his first effort to practice generative questions and positive framing with his team, Ravi discovered the importance of the Anticipatory Principle. Ravi was a senior leader in a large international technology organization headquartered in India. The company operated with a top-down leadership model. In an effort to compete with smaller high-tech startups, the company had invested in AI leadership development with the goal of increasing agility, innovation, and engagement.

Ravi had attended the workshops and saw the value of AI. He wanted his team to be more engaged and feel ownership of the business. He decided to involve them in his project design before he turned the final draft over to the vice president. He had already worked on the design for several months. Now it was all but finalized, and he felt comfortable sharing it. He presented it to his team and asked what he thought was a generative question: "I would like to hear what you have to say about this proposed project before I submit it. What questions or suggestions do you have?"

The team, pleased to be asked, did ask questions and make suggestions, some of which challenged the basic strategy and structure of his plan. Ravi got defensive and began advocating for the plan, explaining why his design was the right one. After a while the team stopped engaging. One of the members

*Hold your viewpoint lightly. Make room for new perspectives.*

whispered to a colleague, "Why did he ask us if he wasn't open to our suggestions? What a waste of time!"

The meeting ended, and Ravi felt that he'd completely failed to implement the AI practices. What had happened? The answer was not in Ravi's questions; it was in what lay behind the questions. Ravi had put in months of work on a design he thought was final. He was anticipating that he would simply get approval from the team, and they would feel good about being asked. The whispering team member identified the issue: a genuinely generative question can be extended only if we are open to hearing and welcoming responses, even those that challenge us.

Had Ravi been open to their responses, he might have asked more questions that could have teased out their thinking and ideas, which could have resulted in changing the design or reinforcing the design he had crafted. For example, Ravi might have responded to the team's questions about his strategy by saying, "Tell me more about your ideas. What do you like most about my proposal, and what suggestions do you have to make it even better?" The responses might have shed light on ideas he hadn't considered, or they might have helped his team learn new information that further strengthened his strategy.

Ravi's situation is not uncommon. When we have invested a lot in something we've created or we deeply believe in, we tend to advocate for it. For this reason, it pays to invite engagement up front in the early stages. Imagine how Ravi might have reacted had he brought his initial thinking to the team after only one week, with the same positive frame and generative questions. Uncommitted to his own outcome and expecting creative ideas, he would have been open to valuable input. This would have generated a very different conversation, most likely one worth having.

Ravi's story illustrates how expectations influence the tone and direction of our conversations. His story began with his belief that his team would approve his plan, and this belief blocked his ability to be open to authentic responses to his questions. Ravi's experience was not unique. In our work with clients, we've discovered that most of us are constantly planning, anticipating, musing, worrying, imagining, thinking, wondering, and assuming. This seemingly passive activity affects our expectations. Those expectations influence the way we see, listen, and talk. When tuning in, taking the time to reflect on our own thinking and expectations helps us stay open to possibilities.

In our last story, Jack also has positive expectations, and he discovers the power of using a positive question to unlock meaningful moments with his children.

## Positive Question, Positive Outcome

*Positive Principle: The more positive and generative the question, the more positive and long-lasting the outcome.*

Jack's story is an all-too-common one among those who have children. Many parents have struggled to engage their children in a conversation about their day by asking the simple, open-ended question "How was school today?" Jack was no different, until he followed the Positive Principle. Jack was a manager in a manufacturing plant who happened to share a more personal story with us. One day he confided, "I do my best to be home in time to tuck my three children in to bed each night. I used to ask them how their day went and if anything happened at school that day. I would always get the same answers: *good* and *nothing*." He shrugged, "How could a child be in school all day and say that nothing happened?" Then he smiled. "One evening, I asked my oldest son, who is eight, a more positive question: 'What was the best thing that happened at school today?'"

"What?" his son replied, alerted by a different question. Jack asked it again. His son thought about it for a moment. His face lit up. He told his dad about how they got to dissect a snake and how cool it was. He also shared that their class earned a special pizza lunch because they had earned the most reading points.

*What is the best thing that happened today?*

Jack anticipated that his children had school stories to share, but he had not been able to surface them. Much to his delight, his generative question changed the tone and direction of his conversations with his children. He learned a lot from this first conversation. He discovered new ways to engage his kids. This eventually led him to try such questions at the plant with his employees, where it was equally successful.

The Positive Principle, sometimes referred to as the Generative Principle, is the idea that the more generative our questions and comments, the more positive our actions and potential. Bold, generative questions, like Jack's, inspire strong, affirmative images. Research shows that we naturally move in the direction of the images that are stimulated by such questions.[8] All the more reason to make them as generative as possible. If we look at each of the stories in this chapter, conversations worth having ultimately depended on the way the person framed or understood the situation and the questions each person asked:

- Alisha: "Tell me, where do you feel you are excelling in each of these areas on your floor?"
- Ms. Wittet: "What are his strengths? When is he most engaged and excited about learning?"
- Ms. Wittet: "What could you say or do to let me know I need to repeat something more clearly the next time?"
- Gabriela: "Are there any faculty who are on board with what you are trying to do?"
- Daniel: "Remember when you were able to stay on the beams and began to move the team across the swamp? What did you do to help you stay on the beams and move as a team?"
- Jack: "What was the best thing that happened at school today?"

The five principles are summarized in Table 5.2.

Everything that we say and do moves us and those around us. Our conversations are governed by these five principles. The next time you find yourself in a conversation, take a moment to tune in and reflect on how these principles are at play. What is different about the principles in action when you are above the line or below? Allow the principles to deepen your ability to tune in and stay open and curious long enough to be surprised and delighted with what emerges. If you do that, then you're on track to be the driver of conversations worth having and arrive at desired destinations.

In the next chapter, we'll explore how to formally use the two practices and five principles to fuel productive and meaningful engagement for both organizational and community change. At the systems level, you can use a formal AI methodology called the 5-D Cycle to initiate whole-system strategic conversations around important and consequential topics.

## Table 5.2 Appreciative Inquiry Principles Summary

| Principle | Essence of the Principle |
|---|---|
| Constructionist Principle | • We jointly construct our social realities through our shared conversations, and then our social reality influences the way we talk.<br>• When we change the way we talk together, the questions we ask, and so on, we change the present reality and future.<br>• *Words create worlds.* |
| Simultaneity Principle | • Change happens the moment we ask the question or the moment we make a comment or enter the conversation.<br>• *Inquiry is intervention.* |
| Poetic Principle | • There are many perspectives, multiple ways of knowing and understanding. How we understand a situation or a person and what story we tell about it affects everything.<br>• *You have a choice in how you see things.* |
| Anticipatory Principle | • We move in the direction of our thoughts and the images that we hold.<br>• What we focus on expands.<br>• *We see what we expect to see; what we look for, we find.* |
| Positive (Generative) Principle | • The questions we ask and what we inquire into are generative. The more positive and generative the questions, the more positive and generative the outcome.<br>• *Positive images and positive actions produce positive results.* |

Note: For more information on the five classic principles of Appreciative Inquiry, see the AI Commons, available at https://appreciativeinquiry.champlain.edu /learn/appreciative-inquiry-introduction/5-classic-principles-ai/.

# 6

# Scaling Up Great Conversations

*A leader is best when people barely know he exists. When his work is done, his aim fulfilled, they will say: We did it ourselves.*
—Lao-Tzu

**When you think** about people having productive and worthwhile conversations, how many individuals do you assume are in the conversation? You probably know intuitively what the research tells us: if there are more than eight to twelve people, you can't really have a meaningful conversation. We know that conversations worth having energize and motivate people. We also know they are productive and meaningful. Imagine the potential for organizations and communities if we could have those kinds of conversations with the whole system!

This potential has already been achieved in cities such as Cleveland and Denver and in countries as different as Nepal and Chile. Contrary to what research would have us believe, these powerful whole-system conversations have taken place with fifty, one hundred, even forty-five hundred people at the same time. They have also happened in thousands of organizations around the world, including Google, Accenture, Verizon, ANZ Bank of Australia, Green Mountain Coffee Roasters, Nutrimental, Bibb County School District (Georgia), Clarke Group, the US Navy, the Cleveland Clinic, World Vision, the United Way

> The people and their conversations are the organization.

of America, and the United Nations Global Compact.[1] One of our favorite organizations is Fairmount Santrol, which has been using Appreciative Inquiry to engage people in worthwhile, whole-system conversations for over fifteen years.[2] Jenniffer Deckard, its CEO, shared the following:

> *We are a flourishing enterprise because of AI. AI is contagious and its principles have so much meaning to our employees. We put it into practice in our meetings, strategy sessions, annual reports, new innovations, and culture. AI applies everywhere and anywhere from our families to our working together to solve complex issues.[3]*

It may be hard to imagine having a great conversation at the system level. Yet it is actually made possible because the AI practices are formalized in a structured process that catalyzes whole-system conversations worth having. The process is called the Appreciative Inquiry 5-D Cycle, named for its five phases: *Define, Discover, Dream, Design,* and *Deploy*. Let's take a look at what happened when this process was used to catalyze a new venture abroad.

Gerard Krupp was president of a German automotive supplier. The company was faced with mounting challenges from its original equipment manufacturers (OEMs) and suppliers in the United States. In addition, it needed a clearer direction, stronger customer relationships, and improved profitability. The solution was to set up a second Technology Center in Michigan to be closer to the automotive OEMs. Gerard was sure that this was the way to meet the multiple demands from his customers. However, he knew that it wouldn't be easy. He had a team of talented, committed, hardworking people who stuck their necks out for him time after time. Asking members of the Technology Center in Germany to pick up their families and move to the United States was going to be a bold move.

For two reasons, Gerard chose Erich to be the program manager to lead the move. Erich had the ability to work across silos. This capability was important because the Technology Center's administration, technology, sales and marketing, and research and development (R&D) teams did not currently collaborate well. Erich was going to have to hire several additional US employees and create a unified team as well as a winning strategy to drive growth. Over the past seven years in Germany, Erich had demonstrated his ability to lead conflicting teams in meaningful dialogues that resulted in win-win outcomes.

For the first thirty days in the new location, the transplanted teams set up shop while anticipating that headquarters would send a game plan for them. As people typically do, those who moved took their current office culture with them. They reproduced the workplace customs and climate they knew, thus being loyal to their functional team. But it was a challenge for the newly hired American employees to find their place in that climate. In general, no one thought to share information or planning outside their own small team. Conversations across those divides were infrequent. When they did occur, they were often critical and destructive.

Meanwhile, Erich knew that he could not wait for corporate to tell them what to do and how to do it. Having attended an AI professional development workshop a few years earlier, Erich planned to unite the separate teams into one that worked collaboratively. He wanted them to focus collectively on increasing existing business and driving new business for the whole organization. He planned to accomplish this by changing the tone and direction of the conversations among team members. To initiate that, he engaged all of them in a center-wide conversation to design a strategic plan using the 5-D Cycle.

Erich knew that the 5-D Cycle would leverage the team's knowledge and experience to create unprecedented change. This more-formal methodology for using generative questions and positive framing to foster strategic conversations promised to unite the Tech Center, eliminate silos, and generate a shared vision and plan for achieving the center's purpose. Since the framing for a systems strategic conversation is just as important as it is for a one-on-one interaction or a meeting, Erich knew it would be important to have the perspectives from each of the different areas as well as both countries involved in creating that frame. So he brought together a representative from each area to form a six-person core team. To enlist them in planning the event, the first thing he did was to explain AI and the 5-D Cycle.[4]

## Overview of the 5-D Cycle

Erich began his first meeting with the core team by saying, "Most of us want to continue to create a company that excels, to feel inspired at work, and to make meaningful contributions. What if we all felt free to innovate and create new possibilities for products, services, and processes that will help shape a bold future for our organization? If I could show you an idea for how we might get to that future, would you join me in making it happen?"

He went on to tell them about his experience with AI. He shared a few stories about how other companies were using it. His core team seemed enthusiastic and curious about how they could proceed. Erich then showed them the 5 Ds (see figure 6.1) and explained what each of the Ds stood for. He explained, "At each phase of the cycle, we'll have worthwhile conversations that will generate meaningful information and creative possibilities for our team and our work together. Those conversations will enable us to identify our strengths and values and to create positive images of our shared future. We will also design pathways to achieve that future and collectively decide how to put those solutions into practice."

Erich noted that, typically, a professional facilitator is engaged to guide the members of the organization through the

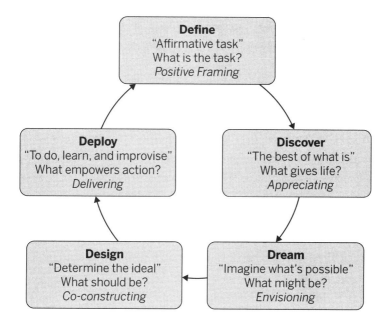

Figure 6.1  Appreciative Inquiry 5-D Cycle

5-D Cycle, freeing all stakeholders to participate in the conversations. He added, "Since I've had training in this process, I'd like us to give it a try without a facilitator. My AI workshop trainer said she would be available to coach or support us from the sidelines. We are small. There are only thirty-four of us. I think we can pull this off together. Are you on board?"

The sales and marketing representative, Joep, responded, "I love your enthusiasm, but I don't really understand what you're asking us to do. I don't know what I'd be saying 'yes' to." Martha, the tech representative, added cynically, "How can thirty-four people have a 'meaningful' conversation?"

"Great question!" replied Erich. "First, most of the conversations are among small groups of six to eight people. Larger group conversation happens when small groups share and merge their ideas. Using this 5-D Cycle will be pretty straightforward for what we are trying to do." Then he went on to explain briefly what the 5 Ds were and how the cycle flowed:

1. In Define, this core planning team will use *positive framing* to clarify the task or focus for our inquiry and to create generative questions that we will ask in the Discover phase.

2. In Discover, we'll engage in one-on-one interviews and small group discussions, based on the questions we crafted in the Define phase. The purpose of this phase is to identify our strengths, which is the *positive core* of our system, along with our purpose and possibilities for the future.

3. In Dream, we'll create shared images of the future, present them in creative and imaginative ways, and write vision statements.

4. In Design, we'll develop prototypes for ways to move toward our vision, leveraging our positive core and staying focused on our mission.

5. In Deploy (sometimes referred to as Destiny or Delivery), we'll revise our prototypes, create action plans, and adopt a learner mindset. This will help us evolve toward our desired future. We will learn and adapt as we move forward by continuously engaging in worthwhile conversations.

Erich asked if there were any questions. Joep asked, "Who will participate in these conversations?" Erich replied, "What if all thirty-four of us participated in the same set of conversations at the same time? If we want to be one united team, then we had better be one team when we discover our strengths, create a vision, and plan our future, don't you think? Are you in?" Erich got a thumbs-up from each representative. The adventure was about to begin!

## Define Phase: Framing the Task and Crafting Generative Questions

Erich had closed the first meeting by asking the core team members to think about why using this approach would be valuable for them. At their next team meeting, Erich opened by asking them, "If you had a chance to think about why this approach would be good to use, what did you come up with?" Each representative had different responses:

- I like the idea of inspiring us to work together and owning this center as a whole team.
- I went back and shared what we talked about with my team, and they really liked the idea of being included in creating our vision and strategic plan. They're excited!
- I think this could make a difference in how we work and the positive impact we could have. It's about time we showed everyone our positive side and our strengths!

Heads were nodding around the table as team members spoke. Erich smiled. He knew how important it was for everyone to be on the same page about *why* they were using this approach. His next question to the group was "What are your highest hopes for the outcome from our conversations?" Erich captured their ideas as they spoke:

- Unity
- Alignment
- Collaboration
- The kind of team that will create unheard-of growth for the company and for our customers
- A shared sense of purpose, direction, and strategy

He was delighted that they had named everything he was hoping for. Erich asked one additional question: "We know our corporate goal: growth from increased sales. What are some of the challenges or issues that we need to address to achieve that?" Again, he captured their comments:

- No one knows exactly what our purpose is; we don't have a mission.
- We don't know where we're going. We don't have a vision!
- And there's no plan, no directive about what we're going to do and how to do it!
- We've never worked as one unified team; I'm not sure we know how to do that. We don't play very well together.
- We don't really know one another's strengths, much less appreciate them.

It was clear to everyone that they needed purpose and direction. Erich framed their next conversation this way: "We know what headquarters wants: help grow the company by increasing sales to current and new customers. That's all we really need to know from them. If there's anything I've learned in life, it's that people commit to what they help create. Let's not wait for instructions from headquarters—let's create our own mission, vision, and strategic plan!" This lit a fire under the core team. "Where do we start?" the R&D representative asked.

"We start by creating a positive frame," Erich replied. "This means clarifying our task for our strategic planning meeting. It will be important for us to identify an affirmative task. That means getting really clear on what we want, or what we want more of, to achieve what the company wants." Erich introduced *flipping* to guide the core team through positive framing. He asked the group to identify the core issue standing in their way of achieving consistent growth. The team landed on this core issue:

- *Name it:* As a center, we have no plan, and we don't know where we're headed, so we can't really work together well.

The team first worked together to identify the positive opposite, and then created the positive frame or affirmative task:

- *Flip it:* We have a plan, we know where we're going, and we work well together.
- *Frame it:* We are a high-performing center with one dynamic team, one vision, one shared mission, and a shared strategic plan.

Just seeing this frame, the core team immediately got excited about future possibilities. Erich suggested, "To accomplish this together, let's make sure we figure out the positive core we bring to becoming a unified, high-performing team. We'll also need a mission and a vision we believe in, as well as a strategy to deliver on our mission. What do you think? Are there other tangible outcomes we want from our meeting?" The core team agreed that those were all that were needed.

Culture and climate emerge from our conversations.

Erich explained that the next step in this phase was crafting questions that would surface positive experiences of high-performance teamwork, key employee strengths, central purpose, and values that would support the center as one team. This would clarify their positive core. They needed to craft two sets of questions. The first step was to devise questions as a guide for one-on-one interviews. Erich showed them a set of classic AI interview questions to help all of them think through the questions they needed to craft (see table 6.1).

The core team worked a long time, putting great care into ensuring that questions were positively framed to elicit stories and conversations that would help the team discover their true potential. The questions also needed to help them learn more about the organization and think through their ultimate purpose. Their final interview guide contained these five questions:

1. Describe a high-point experience working as a team in the Technology Center or organization—a time when you felt most alive and engaged as a member of the team.

**Table 6.1** Five Classic Questions for an Appreciative Inquiry Interview

| | |
|---|---|
| **The first three questions focus on the best of what _is_.** | 1. What would you describe as a high-point experience you have had in your organization?<br>2. What do you value most about yourself, your work, and your organization?<br>3. What gives life to your organization? |
| **The next question focuses on what _might be_, or possibilities.** | 4. Imagine that it's three years later from now, and everything you ever hoped possible is happening at your organization. What's going on? How have things changed? |
| **The final question helps transition to what _can be_.** | 5. What three wishes do you have to enhance the health and vitality of your organization? |

2. What is it that you value about yourself, your colleagues, and the organization?
3. When our center is at its best, what are the core factors (our strengths) that give it life, without which the center would simply not be at its best?
4. Imagine that three years from now the company has grown significantly. Describe the ways in which we work together as one team and how that has enabled the Tech Center to contribute to the organization's success. What business segment(s), technical product(s), or process innovation(s) have been successfully created and launched?
5. What three wishes do you have to strengthen our center or the organization itself?

Erich explained, "After the one-on-one interviews, groups of six to eight people will come together and interviewers will share the high points of their partner's stories, not their own. This will encourage people to listen for understanding and help build positive relationships. Our next task is to design those conversations. We need to structure them so small groups can tease out important themes and ideas from their interviews." The core team came up with the following instructions:

1. *Discover.* Share the highlights of your partner's answer to question 1 and what stood out for you from questions 2 and 3. Capture the ideas so that everyone can see them. After everyone has shared, have a conversation as a group about key themes that emerged. Identify important values and strengths.
2. *Discover.* Based on our core values and strengths, write a brief but focused mission statement.
3. *Dream.* Share your partner's vision of our Technology Center in three years. What stood out for you that was exciting or inspiring? Capture everyone's ideas so others can see them. Once everyone has shared, have a conversation about our future. Create a shared vision for the Tech Center.
4. *Dream.* Share your partner's three wishes. Capture them so that everyone can see them.

After this meeting, the core team seemed very happy with how they had defined the upcoming strategic planning meeting. Erich told them that at their next meeting they would set a date and design the flow for the meeting.

When the core team regrouped the following week, Erich explained how the meeting would flow through the remaining 4 Ds: Discover, Dream, Design, and Deploy. Their focus for this last Define phase meeting was to design the agenda, using the remaining four phases, and also to create any further instructions for small-group conversations and planning. They followed with a logistics plan, divided up responsibilities, and left excited to generate enthusiasm among the other members of their teams.

## A Look Inside Their Strategic Planning Meeting: The 4 Ds

All thirty-four employees gathered for a one-day strategic planning session.[5] Erich opened by reading the following statement:

> *Our company made the investment to move all of us to this office in Michigan to be near our key customers, instilling in us the charge to drive more growth for our organization.*
>
> *There is no guarantee that we will have business tomorrow, and it won't simply be waiting on our doorstep just because we are here now. In the past sixty days, it became clear to me that we have an opportunity and responsibility to create our future and not wait for corporate to tell us what to do.*
>
> *We must realize it is a privilege to be the supplier of choice, and it is our responsibility to be the best at what we do to make it happen. Today, we shall discover our center's strengths—what we do best. We will create a mission statement and guiding vision that inspire and clarify our purpose and direction. We will wrap up this session knowing what we do best, how we best work together, and what our unique value offering is. This will allow us to dive deeper into our core strengths and enable us to create opportunities and design strategic goals and objectives with a collaborative action plan for a shared, preferred future with measurable results.*
>
> *Today, we are part of a team that has been responsible for approximately $60 million in annual revenue. Tomorrow, let us be the team that leads this company to the top of our industry.*
>
> *We need to be innovative and inspire each other into action. Let's create our future as a high-performing center—one dynamic team, one vision, one shared plan. Are you in?*

### Discover Phase: Appreciating What Gives Life

The meeting started with one-on-one interviews, using the questions the core team had crafted. To build relationships and knowledge across silos, the core team asked people to pair up with someone they did not know or work with regularly. Following the interviews, interview pairs formed small groups of six or eight. Guided by the Discover instructions (see page 124), people shared their interview partner's story and what stood out for them as key concepts and ideas related to the task. Then, each group identified common themes from their stories and drafted a mission statement. Each small group shared their themes and mission statement with the larger group. The large group sorted the themes and chose those that they believed made up their positive core for a unified team with one plan and one vision. Later, over lunch, a small group of people merged the ideas from the mission statements into a single shared statement.

Erich and the core team could feel the excitement in the room; the energy was palpable. People were talking across silos, learning about each other, and identifying important concepts that would grow their capacity to thrive as a center while also contributing to organizational success. The Discover phase of their meeting surfaced the following values, strengths, and mission for moving to a state where the center would be a unified, high-performing team:

*Values:* Dedication, flexibility, creativity, innovation, team spirit, and continuous communications. These values are how we will work collaboratively.

*Strengths:*

1. Adaptability: We are highly flexible to deal with change and challenges.
2. Dedication to customers: "That's why we moved here." We will continue to exceed internal and external customer expectations.
3. Strong product core: We can supply uniquely optimized sealants and adhesives.
4. Top-Notch employees: Our employees are highly capable and are up to date in their fields.

Based on six core values and four strengths, the five groups converged on the following mission statement:

*We are a dedicated and flexible team that designs, develops, and provides cost-effective and innovative engineering, NVH [noise, vibration, harshness], sealant, and adhesive solutions that are manufactured to your specifications. We do this in a safe working environment where we retain top-quality employees.*

The room was buzzing; people were talking about how affirming and inspiring this approach was and what great conversations they were having with people they didn't really know. Erich introduced the next activity on the agenda: the Dream phase. He explained, "We don't need to identify weaknesses and threats because we know them. That's why we relocated. We need to come up with a way to inspire each of us to support our customers' and prospective customers' needs and anticipated needs. That begins with dreaming big!"

### Dream Phase: Envisioning What Might Be

Guided by the Dream instructions (see page 124), the same small groups drew on and amplified their positive core to create shared images of the future. Their conversations centered on what might be a chance to envision the organization at its best, the ideal high-performing center team, and a community where all members could flourish. Imagining a desired future and creating literal images shifted people from abstract thinking to creative possibilities, freeing them to explore a shared vision.

The core team had designed this activity to encourage playfulness and inspiration. Small groups created skits and posters. These gave everyone a tangible, sensory understanding of new ways of working together. They also each crafted a written statement to accompany their visual. The vision statements were short, catchy, affirmative, and inspirational.

The whole room came alive with laughter, excitement, and potential during the presentations. To move toward a shared vision that represented the whole group, they did a Vision Walk, an exercise in which everyone reviewed the images and vision statements and then placed sticky dots on those vision statements with which they resonated most. During lunch, a second small group merged the high-dot-count visions into a single image and vision statement, and the group confirmed it:

*To be the global leader providing best-in-class engineering, NVH, sealant, and adhesive solutions with exceptional customer service that exceeds our customers' expectations on time.*

The energy and synergy created during this phase carried participants into the Design phase after lunch. This was when they identified strategies and actions to make their vision a reality.

### Design Phase: Co-constructing What Should Be

After lunch, the group did a gallery walk to look at all that had been generated earlier. They were tasked with identifying ideas that called out to them, opportunities that triggered their passions. Then they generated possibilities: strategies and actions for achieving their dream. People self-organized into small groups around these possibility topics. The first thing they did was clarify the possibility by writing a descriptive statement that captured the contribution this initiative would make to the company. Next, they designed a prototype. Starting with a prototype freed people to see that they didn't have to wait for permission or have to get things exactly right before they could present ideas. Instead, there in the meeting they could design and test their initial thinking. The core team had created some great questions to stimulate small-group design conversations:

- How will we make this happen easily?
- At this moment, what can we design rapidly and test with our colleagues?
- What's the story we would like to tell about how we will do this?
- If we were creating a business to do only this one thing, what would that business be, and what product or service would it provide?

A techie from one of the groups smiled and said, "This is like a *hackathon*." If she meant that this activity was to "hack" the current ways of doing and thinking to make room for creativity and innovation, she was right.

When it was time to share prototypes with the whole, Erich felt blown away by the creativity and knowledge base that had emerged. One team created a new sales call protocol that bridged every team, from product design to delivery. Another team created an innovative process to bring potential clients to the Technology Center to see firsthand how the firm develops custom solutions. After each presentation, Erich invited the rest of the group to provide feedforward—a new concept the core team was introducing: What resonates for me (what do I like about it)? What did I notice? What suggestions do I have to make it even better?

The day was almost over. The outcomes from this Design phase set the stage for taking action. Implementing these prototypes and getting started on tasks were in the next phase of the 5-D cycle.

### Deploy Phase: Living into Empowering Action

Each group gathered for a final conversation about how to *deliver* or *deploy* their prototype. They created written plans with action steps that would move their prototype into reality.

In closing, Erich reflected on the day and how excited he felt with the outcomes. He graciously thanked the members of the planning team and explicitly drew attention to how carefully they had used generative questions and positive framing throughout their design. He spent a little time sharing these two practices with everyone, encouraging them to continue to inspire great conversations as they rolled out their plans and worked together to achieve their goals. Then he invited all those present to tell a brief story about the best thing that happened today and their commitment to taking action.

Deployment continued as people engaged in daily work following the meeting. That day inspired a whole new way of engaging in conversation. Relationships had been formed across the silos, and commitment both to one another and to their shared vision had been strengthened. The core team remained champions for the vision and mission. They made sure prototypes had the support and resources they needed to move forward.

Erich reported back to Gerard in Germany, "The conversations that took place to create the center's mission, vision, and strategic plan went beyond my expectations. The various divisions have become boundaryless in this new Tech Center. I guess that's what happens when people co-create a shared purpose, vision, and plan of action. We are on fire to deliver on our plan!" Everyone was heard; everyone had a stake.

Within ninety days of launching the plan, the tech team saw improved results in productivity, sales, and communications. Morale for the new center had risen to an all-time high, and a positive feeling of a home-away-from-the-corporate-home emerged. A team-based mentality was focusing on continuous improvement, using a results-driven mindset. The members' ability to act so successfully on the outcomes from their planning meeting was the result of their commitment to practice generative questions and positive framing as ways of being and working together.

This was the first time that any division of the company had created a strategic plan based on *all* employees' insights, not only those of a few senior leaders. Gerard took notice of the results. He phoned Erich to ask him, "What made this relocation project a success?" Erich paused for a moment and replied, "I think it's because our strategic conversations were inclusive. Everyone mattered. Conversations centered on how we could make this a great success. People were invited to share their best selves, and the conversations unleashed the momentum to become a unified, winning team. Everyone knows that we can achieve the tasks ahead because they co-created them!"

Gerard then asked, "Erich, can you teach me how to create these kinds of conversations back at corporate? We need to ignite the potential of everyone in this organization." Erich smiled and replied, "I'd be delighted. It will be easy to teach you generative questions and positive framing to help you have meaningful conversations and possibly even to guide department-size planning meetings. However, if you're talking about a whole-organization effort, I think we'll need a professional AI facilitator."

What made this process relatively easy for Erich to use was his applied understanding of the two basic practices, his attention to the principles, his past experience with the 5-D structured approach, and coaching from his AI trainer. Table 6.2 summarizes what Erich and his core team did for the Technology Center. You can do it with your division or department as well. Just keep in mind what inspired Erich. He assumed that the responsibility for change resided with all the people in the center. He realized that the people and their conversations *are* the organization. They create the culture and climate in the way they talk and work together. Real organizational change begins when the people are invited to take responsibility for the system by engaging in productive, worthwhile conversations about their shared future.

Organizations and communities are socially constructed systems. People designed the structures, processes, workflows, and policies that are in place. So make sure those systems are supporting the outcomes you want. The 5-D Cycle enables people to have strategic conversations to identify and amplify the *best of what is* in a system, to continuously create the *best*

Table 6.2 Appreciative Inquiry 5-D Cycle: Phases and Activities

| 5-D Cycle Phase | Activities |
| --- | --- |
| Phase 1: Define | 1. Frame the task.<br>2. Craft the interview guide and small-group discussion (see table 6.1 for generative AI questions).<br>3. Design how to implement phases 2 through 5. |
| Phase 2: Discover | 1. Engage in interviews, using the guide.<br>2. Share and analyze the stories in small groups, identifying the positive core, opportunities, and possibilities. |
| Phase 3: Dream | 1. Envision the future grounded in the positive core.<br>2. Create shared images that ignite your sensory imagination.<br>3. Craft word images that align with the visual images. |
| Phase 4: Design | 1. Generate possibilities for achieving the dream.<br>2. Craft possibility statements.<br>3. Engage in rapid prototyping. |
| Phase 5: Deploy | 1. Craft action plans.<br>2. Enlist champions and commitment.<br>3. Take action.<br>4. Engage in cycles of prototyping and learning.<br>5. Value (not evaluate) the progress that has been made and inquire into what made it possible. |

*of what can be,* and to design *how it can be,* which often means changing structures and systems. The result is that people come alive and formally commit to the future of the organization or community. Why? You'll find out in the next chapter, where you'll learn how the practice of using generative questions and positive framing affects us in ways that support our work and our lives in general.

# 7

# It's Not Magic, It's Science!

*No matter what people tell you, words and ideas can change the world.*
—Nancy H. Kleinbaum

**If the experience** of our clients, families, and colleagues detailed in the stories in this book has not convinced you that there is magic in conversations worth having, then perhaps the evidence from more than thirty-five years of scientific research will help explain how generative questions and positive framing bring forth the best in human nature. This research falls into three distinct areas: neuroscience,[1] positive image/position action, and positive psychology.[2] The net outcome of this research points to the importance of using language to inspire positive emotions, positive images, and positive actions. Science tells us to follow the 80/20 rule—a ratio of 80 percent positive emotions and imagery to 20 percent negative—to support well-being and excellence at the individual, group, and organization levels.[3] We'll begin with neuroscience.

### Neuroscience

In 1990, the invention of functional magnetic resonance imaging (fMRI) enabled neuroscientists to see and measure brain activity. The technology allowed scientists to see what happens to our neurophysiology under different conditions. Researchers could engage people in different kinds of conversations and activities and detect what was going on with their brain chemistry by measuring changes in blood flow. Neurological brain research has shown that strong beliefs and imagery actually change brain chemistry.[4] It also has shown that brain chemistry influences our response to a given stimulus.

For example, Tony, an accountant for a small accounting firm, recently had an argument with his boss that left him believing he is going to be fired. He also knows that without his income, his family can't make its mortgage. These beliefs create a neural "preset" that has him wired to react negatively when his wife suggests they go out to dinner. Had he instead had an experience with his boss that left him sure he was going to get a raise, he would have been delighted to go out to dinner with his wife. This is where tuning in can help us better respond to the world around us. We have the ability to influence our brain chemistry simply by pausing, taking several deep breaths, and getting curious. This allows us to choose our response even in potentially inflammatory situations. It was for exactly this reason that the Los Angeles Police Department Drug Task Force received special training to handle drug busts.

The task force was about to make a drug bust. Its members were on-site, adrenaline pumping, ready for the signal to rush a building. The chief gave a hand signal, but no one moved. Instead, all the officers began to breathe slowly, recalling a time when they felt deeply appreciative or grateful. They envisioned that time, recalling the imagery, the conversations, and especially the feelings. After this brief practice, the captain nodded his head and the squad then rushed the building. They broke through the door and subdued everyone present without a single shot. The arrest was a success. The situation and their beliefs about it did not change, but their pre-rush (pre-framing) practice changed their brain chemistry. The change enabled them to better respond to the tense situation they were about to encounter.[5]

*Positive emotions broaden and build our capacity.*

The police had practiced a technique they learned from the HeartMath Institute, a practice grounded in the institute's neurological research.[6] The institute discovered that using positive imagery plus recalling positive experiences can bring the nervous system into coherence. Coherence produces a brain chemistry that allows more complete access to the neocortex, which is where all reasoning and critical thinking take place. Before their training, when the police prepared for a drug bust, adrenaline and images of chaos and violence created a brain chemistry in them that was less coherent and highly reactive. The result was typically a more chaotic scene, one more likely to erupt with violence and even shootings and possibly deaths. In a coherent state, police officers were better able to assess the scene and respond without escalating the potential for violence.

When it comes to conversations, critical or destructive ones are most often perceived as threats. A threat changes brain chemistry. It routes more oxygen and nutrition to the part of our brain responsible for keeping us safe. The greater the fear, the more oxygen is sent to support our fight-or-flight response, and the less oxygen is available for the prefrontal lobe and neocortex. Having a strong sense of safety, connection, and belonging does the opposite: oxygen and nutrients flow to all parts of the brain and nervous system, supporting high performance. Generative questions and positive framing stimulate the kind of brain chemistry that enables people to live and work at optimal capacity, which is what most of us desire in any relationship, organization, or community.

The HeartMath Institute's research shows that recalling experiences of deep appreciation, gratitude, and unconditional love are the most effective for creating coherence.[7] When we frame a conversation positively and ask generative questions of others, we are, in effect, stimulating coherence for everyone participating in the conversation. Furthermore, if we are following the Positive Principle and asking powerful generative questions, we are also inspiring positive and bold images. The research on imagery further supports the value of fostering conversations worth having.

### Positive Image/Positive Action

If you found the story about the Los Angeles Drug Task Force memorable, it might be because it created an image in your mind. Research has shown that imagery is compelling. It supports long-term memory and influences us to move in the direction of the images we hold.[8] Brain research shows that we process language in different parts of the brain, and the whole brain is necessary for comprehension (see figure 7.1). In an fMRI, imagery lights up more of our right brain,

**Figure 7.1 Right Brain/Left Brain Neural Processing Centers**
Drawing by Caryn Brownelle Hanna, Graphic Facilitation and Illustration, CarynDHarma @gmail.com

and abstract concepts light up the left.[9] The corpus callosum, which connects the two hemispheres, enables us to understand concepts that contain both abstract words and image words.

What is striking is that imagery often trumps both intention *and* understanding. Children know what teachers mean when they say, "Don't run in the hall!" For some children, however, the "run in the hall" is overwhelmingly compelling and that is all they hear. So they take off running, leaving a dumbfounded teacher behind. This is why it is more effective to tell children what you *want* them to do rather than what you *don't*. Teachers have more success when they say, "Please walk." That can be an equally compelling image.

The right brain doesn't register the difference between fantasy and reality; an image is just an image. This research has inspired many athletes and coaches to integrate visualization into their practice. It turns out that visualizing a perfect free throw for 50 percent of one's practice time results in higher performance than practicing the throw for 100 percent of the time.[10] As David Cooperrider states, "We are recognizing that the power of positive imagery is not just some popular illusion or wish but an expression of the mind's capacity for shaping reality."[11] This is highly relevant for both team and organization leaders.

Shared imagery can be a powerful driver for action. As you read in chapter 6, during the Dream phase, Erich and his Technology Center team intentionally created a shared vision to support a unified team, all working for the same outcomes. Imagery also lies at the heart of generative questions and positive framing. The Positive Principle draws on the power of imagery. Powerfully positive questions generate images, which compel us to action.

Given this, it is both logical and practical to intentionally focus conversations on what you want. Much of the time, focusing conversations on problems is not worthwhile because the associated imagery does not move us away from the problem. By contrast, the practice of using generative questions and positive framing creates images of where we want to move and what we want to achieve. Such conversations have the potential to generate powerfully positive images that compel us toward desired outcomes. *These are conversations worth having.*

It is not a new idea that positive images influence our future. Research across diverse disciplines has demonstrated that positive images generate positive action for individuals, groups, and organizations. You may be familiar with these areas of research:

- *The Placebo Effect.*[12] The belief that a pill will heal generates neurophysiological conditions in the brain and body that literally support healing. Conversations about healing an unhealthy relationship or a dysfunctional organizational climate are no different. Appreciative conversations inspire belief in the possibility of a strong and loving relationship or a climate where people thrive. Such conversations alter brain chemistry, giving us greater capacity to bring those desired futures into reality. Recall Daniel's work with the First Nations gang members. His belief about the power of positive framing and curiosity led him to ask generative questions that surfaced what he could not see before. What strong beliefs do *you* hold that positively influence your ability to thrive?

- *The Pygmalion Effect.*[13] The beliefs and images that we hold about others can affect the lives of those others. If a manager believes an employee can succeed, for example, the employee is much more likely to do so. The manager's belief encourages her to see the employee's potential and to provide the necessary support for his success. In addition, others see that dynamic and are influenced in how they see the employee. In turn, this influences neurophysiological coherence, giving the employee access to his full capacity to do well, even in challenging situations. Recall Jamal's experience of being in Ms. Summers's and Ms. Wittit's classes. His success or failure was directly correlated with their beliefs about him. The Pygmalion Effect and the Placebo Effect can work together to produce even greater positive results. Daniel and his young men are a case in point. His belief in the facilitation process led him to ask questions that resulted in his ability to see the strengths in the gang members. In turn, his belief in them inspired them to bring forth their leadership and teamwork ability to be successful in their activities. How are *your* beliefs about members of your family and workplace affecting their ability to thrive?

- *Positive Affect, Positive Effect.*[14] The words we use have an immediate impact on neurophysiology, our own as well as others'. The tone and direction of our conversation can influence the brain chemistry of those around us. Generative questions and positive framing influence neurophysiological coherence and make room for the full potential of individuals to come forth. This is exactly what Ms. Wittit did for Jamal. Daniel's shift to generative questions had an immediate effect on the boys. Gabriela's question to the provost caused an immediate shift in his neurophysiology, which showed up in his expression and the change in tone and direction of the conversation. See if you can have a positive impact on others' affect today, merely by asking a generative question.

The idea that positive framing is correlated with our capacity to thrive is not new. Norman Vincent Peale and

Zig Ziglar had touted this since the 1940s and '50s.[15] Some naysayers have dismissed their ideas as fluff. However, turn-of-the-twenty-first-century technology has given us the ability to actually correlate neurophysiological chemistry with these ideas. Hard science now validates the value of positive framing and holding a positive attitude. The benefits for organizations and relationships are further underscored by research in the area of positive psychology.

### Positive Psychology

When we engage in conversations worth having, the telltale signs are energy, creativity, and positive emotions. Research in the field of positive psychology shows that positive emotions correlate with an individual's capacity for high performance and cooperation. In the late 1990s, Barbara Fredrickson's pioneering research into the then-emerging field of positive psychology demonstrated that positive emotions broaden and build our capacity for higher-order thinking, creativity, empathy, cooperation, resilience, and connection.[16]

Over the last twenty years, Fredrickson's research has underscored the benefits of positivity, which is the practice of being positive or optimistic in attitude. Engaging in thoughts, behaviors, and activities that produce positive emotions actually expands our thought repertoire and increases creativity.[17] Positive emotions include more than merely joy and happiness. Fredrickson identified many emotions that generate positivity, including interest, curiosity, hope, gratitude, kindness, surprise (the pleasant type), confidence, enthusiasm, satisfaction, inspiration, awe, love, and more.

Conversations that value and connect people, uncover what *is* working, and stimulate images of the ideal future foster many of these emotions. Fredrickson's seminal study, "What Good Are Positive Emotions?," and her book that followed, *Positivity*, support the idea that positivity creates an upward spiral of confidence and optimism.[18] This upward spiral improves health and well-being. It also expands our capacity for change, growth, learning, effective relationships, and solution-finding. Her more recent research demonstrates that conversations worth having support what she refers to as "positivity resonance," which is that "energizing micro-moment when you truly connect with someone else."[19] Such moments increase our physical, emotional, and mental health and unlock the performance capacity of teams. This is exactly what every organization is looking for. The good news: the potential for positivity and positivity resonance exist within every organization and community. The even better news: you can bring out that best in every person, fueling productive and meaningful engagement through generative questions and positive framing.

Organization leaders will be especially interested in the research of Marcial Losada and Emily Heaphy, who studied organization teams.[20] They looked at the impact conversations had on team performance. They measured impact by looking at profit and loss, customer satisfaction, and 360-degree reviews. They listened in on team conversations and calculated the ratio of positive to negative interactions, inquiry versus advocacy statements, and a focus on self versus others. The results were profound (see table 7.1). A 6:1 ratio of positive to negative interactions for high performance teams is a prescription for effective group dynamics. It is also not surprising, given the scientific research on neurophysiology and performance.

Table 7.1 Results of Losada and Heaphy's Research

| Type of Talk | High-Performance Teams | Low-Performance Teams |
|---|---|---|
| Positive to Negative | 6:1 | 1:20 |
| Inquiry vs. Advocacy | 1:1 | 1:3 |
| Self vs. Other | 1:1 | 30:1 |

This link between our interactions and the outcomes is true not only at work. John Gottman's research on what makes a marriage succeed suggests that there is a *magic ratio* of 5:1, positive to negative interactions. He found that marriages are significantly more likely to succeed when the couple's interactions are near that 5:1 ratio of positive to negative. When the ratio approaches 1:1, marriages move rapidly toward divorce.[21]

Gottman tested his magic ratio by predicting a couple's future based on their interactions. In 1992, he videotaped a fifteen-minute conversation between the members of seven hundred couples, counting the number of positive and negative interactions. He followed up with each couple ten years later. He had predicted divorce with 94 percent accuracy![22] If we were to overhear fifteen minutes of conversation among *your* team members or family, what might we predict?

In addition to strengthening relationships and giving us greater access to our broader capacity, Appreciative Inquiry–based conversations invite meaningful engagement and often lead to action that gives us a sense of accomplishment. Martin Seligman, who is frequently credited with initiating this domain of psychology,[23] sees the topic of positive psychology as "well-being, that the gold standard for measuring well-being is flourishing, and that the goal of positive psychology is to increase flourishing."[24] Seligman suggests that the pathway to flourishing is to increase positive emotion, engagement, meaning, positive relationships, and accomplishments (PERMA).[25] These are metrics associated with conversations worth having. If you aspire to helping your organization flourish, one pathway is to ensure that the nature of the workplace conversations you have are predominantly appreciative and inquiry-based.

If you want strong relationships, high-performance teams, and a successful organization, then simply use the two basic AI practices. The research underscores the importance of having worthwhile or affirming conversations *most of the time*. It does not mean all the time. There are going to be negative interactions and situations that result in negative emotions. That's okay. Fredrickson's research suggests that a 3:1 positive to negative ratio is sufficient to maintain positivity. Losada and Heaphy's research showed that a 6:1 ratio is needed for high-performance teams. And Gottman says it is 5:1 for successful relationships. The point in understanding these various results is that we should maintain a healthy imbalance between positive and negative interactions. Remember Elizabeth and Ram's first reaction to Kamal when he told them there was a problem? They felt embarrassed for not being "good enough." What enabled them to rise to the occasion rather than collapsing in despair was the resilience they had built from many positive interactions, plus Kamal's Appreciative Inquiry–based approach to jointly creating a solution. We recommend aiming for a 4:1 ratio. This is a ratio with which we are all familiar: the 80/20 rule.[26]

Whether you are inspired by the compelling stories in this book or convinced by scientific evidence, or both, it is clear that if you want to inspire the best in human nature, it makes sense to practice generative questioning and positive framing. The bottom line is that conversations worth having are within your reach. You can intentionally expand your capacity to thrive by tuning in, even in an uncertain world. In our last chapter, you'll see how it's possible to do precisely that, any time, any place, and in any situation.

# 8

# Any Time, Any Place, Any Situation

*Your conversations help create your world. Speak of delight, not dissatisfaction. Speak of hope, not despair. Let your words bind up wounds, not cause them.*

—Tao Te Ching

**Appreciative Inquiry** is a strengths-based, enlivening approach used to discover the best in people, organizations, and the communities around them. AI research has shown that systems (of self, teams, organizations, and communities) move in the direction of the questions people ask. AI initiates positive emotions and opens the doorway to unimagined possibilities for those who experience this way of being in and making sense of the world. This way of being is perhaps best described by Jane Magruder Watkins, who was a senior AI practitioner, organization development consultant, and author, who said, AI is "a habit of mind, heart, and imagination that searches for the success, the life-giving force rather than disaster and despair."[1] Starting appreciative and inquiry-based conversations is basically a matter of tuning in and choosing to use the two simple practices: asking generative questions and creating a positive frame. When following the AI principles becomes second nature, you will naturally initiate productive and meaningful interactions most of the time.

### Getting Started with the Basic Practices

We have invited you to develop a new conversation habit, which depends upon your ability to be intentional with your words. The single most important way to start fostering conversations worth having is to tune in on a regular basis. The following are some exercises to help you get started.

1. *Tune in:* Pause, breathe, and get curious on a regular basis. Ask yourself, "Where am I? Where is the other person? What am I curious about? What do I want to happen?" The more aware you are of your present body-mindset, the more capable you are of being deliberate with your words, tone, and intent.

2. *Observe conversations at home and work:* Try this exercise for at least a day before you start intentionally practicing generative questions and positive framing (though it might be hard to stop yourself if you've read this far!):

   • Get an index card and label one side "positive" and the reverse side "negative." After each conversation you observe or have (regardless of how long or short and whether you are observing others or having a conversation with yourself or someone else), put a tick mark on the side representing whether it was an appreciative (positive) or a depreciative (negative) conversation. If it was a conversation you participated in, jot down a couple of words to remind yourself of how you felt during and after the interaction and whether it was worthwhile overall. If it was a conversation you observed, write down a few notes about where you were and what the tone and the direction of the interaction were. Note your observation of people's body language.

- At the end of the day, reflect on your conversations and those you observed. You might also reflect on how you feel about the day and what you've accomplished.

- You can calculate your positivity ratio by adding up the total positive versus negative conversations you had. If your ratio is less than 3:1, it's time to change your conversations. Fortunately, there's a simple way to do that!

- Do you notice a difference between the nature of the conversations you have with yourself, your family, and others?

3. *Notice the difference between problem-solving and Appreciative Inquiry:* If you're an effective problem-solver, you've probably been rewarded for that quality throughout your life. We are not suggesting that you give up this very effective skill. Rather, we ask you to be aware of when an appreciative approach might be more effective. We invite you to experience the difference between finding a solution using a more traditional problem-solving approach and using an appreciative approach. To confirm the power of this comparison, try the following exercise several times today or tomorrow:

- When you are with people, consciously identify problems. Come up with solutions or ask problem-solving questions. Observe others' reactions and responses. Problem-solving questions typically entail asking about what's wrong, what's not working, and why. Notice the dynamics of these conversations. Observe subtle body language, as well as the tone and direction of the conversation. Along these same lines, if someone presents you with a problem, begin brainstorming solutions and notice how the conversation flows.

- Then, consciously shift toward a positive frame by asking generative questions. Generative questions seek to make the invisible visible, create shared understanding, generate new knowledge, and expand possibility. If someone else suggests the problem, ask them a generative question to flip the focus—for example, "This project is never going to work with the way it's designed." A generative question might be "What changes could we make so it *would* work?" Again, notice what happens to the dynamics of the conversation. Pay attention to changes in body language, the energy level, and the tone and direction of the conversation. This can be especially powerful when someone presents you with a problem they are trying to solve. It might be helpful to first find out what they really want.

- What emotions and feelings do these different ways of engaging in conversations generate—for you and for others? If you're a great problem-solver, such conversations might be energizing for you. What about others in the conversation? Which of these approaches builds stronger relationships among everyone? Makes room for everyone? Inspires the most innovative solutions?

## Life-Changing Outcomes

The following are examples of ways people engage in conversation both before and after they learn about the two practices. Which ones are conversations worth having?

### *With Yourself*

*Before:* Why didn't I get more accomplished today? How will I ever get this done if I don't take it home? I am exhausted but need to bring the report home with me. I am so tired of working at home every night. It's got to get done, and there's no one else to help me and no way I'll be ready for the meeting at 10:00 a.m.

*After:* I need to get this report finished by tomorrow, and today is gone! How can I be the most effective and efficient in knocking this thing out by 10 a.m. tomorrow? What will it take to finish it? I can just get here early tomorrow morning; that will do it!

### *With Your Partner/Spouse*

*Before:* I'm not happy. You're always exhausted, and I'm tired of just watching TV. Why don't we ever do anything?

*After:* You know, we used to do more things together, and I really loved those times. I miss them. Remember when we _____? What would it take to start doing some of those things again?

### With Your Children

*Before:* Why aren't you home on time? You've got to stop getting in so late at night after curfew. Perhaps grounding you for a week is what you need!

*After:* I really need you to be in by curfew. We have good reasons for wanting you home by that time. Not to mention that I worry when you don't make it in. Sometimes you *do* manage to get here on time. What is it about those occasions that enables you to get home on time? How can we make sure that happens more often? I want to know you are safe. What can we both do to make sure I don't worry if you're running late?

### With Colleagues

*Before:* These missed deadlines are a real problem for the department. Why are you late? If you can't do the work, we can give it to someone who can.

*After:* Do you agree that when we get our projects accomplished efficiently and on time we're in a better position to achieve our goals? What do you need to help you make sure your work on the project is completed on time?

### With Government

*Before:* Why is there so much divisiveness between our citizens?

*After:* Which organizations are working to bridge the divide in this country? How can we bring that activity to our own community?

Simply altering the way in which you frame a situation and the questions you ask will change any interaction *and* the outcome. To generate big change and worthwhile outcomes, generative questions and positive framing have proven themselves, even in the most difficult of situations. At the time of our writing this book, many seeds of division and negativity are being sown into our national and global conversations. It is our hope that you might become a sower of conversations worth having in your communities and workplaces, especially across the polar divides that have emerged. This is where asking generative questions and practicing positive framing can actually begin to mend and even strengthen the fabric of our communities and nations, within and across our borders.

This may mean looking for the opportunity or the means to bring out the best even in a bad situation. It may also mean asking, "What is of value in this terrible thing that happened?" It may require first that you reflect on your own beliefs and ways of understanding, and then that you open the door for something new and meaningful to emerge. The AI principles will guide you here.

## Playing by the Rules

Principles are "fundamental rules or truths that have application across the wide field of human interaction and engagement."[2] The principles introduced in chapter 5 are true, whether we are aware of them or not. They are true, regardless of our actions. They can be predictive of the outcomes of our actions. Their predictive nature is what makes them valuable. When we become aware of the principles, we can use them to enhance our ability to foster meaningful engagement.

You are likely to first bump up against the principles as you start to practice generative questions and positive framing. If you recall, Ravi at the tech company in India had a positive frame and asked generative questions, yet he ended up in a depreciative conversation. He bumped up against the principles—the rules. Successful application of the practices means following these principles to help you align your thoughts and feelings with your framing, language, and desired outcomes. Remember the following about the AI principles:

1. *Constructionist Principle:* Understanding, interpersonal dynamics, meaning, and ultimately our social reality are created through language and in conversation. Playing by this rule means
   - Reflecting on the meaning you are bringing to an interaction
   - Choosing to hold your viewpoint lightly and staying open
   - Choosing words that allow for the creation of new meaning and understanding with others

2. *Simultaneity Principle:* Change happens the moment a question is asked or a statement is made. Playing by this rule means
   - Being mindful of your words and choosing language that aligns with your intentions
   - Paying attention to how your words are affecting yourself and others
   - Asking generative questions to clarify other people's intention behind their words instead of simply reacting to them

3. *Poetic Principle:* Every person, organization, or situation can be seen and understood from many perspectives. Playing by this rule means

- Staying open and avoiding judgment
- Recognizing that what you are focused on is only part of the picture
- Attending to possibilities (instead of delving deeply into "fixing" things), moments of joy (instead of ruminating on fear or worry), and sources of energy and momentum (instead of inertia)
- Recognizing that you have a choice in how you interpret what happens in your life

4. *Anticipatory Principle:* The images and thoughts we hold influence our intention and conversation. Playing by this rule means
   - Expecting positive outcomes
   - Anticipating what you want instead of fearing what you *don't* want
   - Looking for the opportunity, the good, the true, and the beautiful

5. *Positive Principle:* The more positive and generative the question, the more positive and long-lasting the outcomes. Playing by this rule means
   - Asking bold, generative questions that elicit strong, affirmative images of possibility

These principles reinforce the idea that everything we think, say, and do moves us and those around us in one way or another. These principles underscore and drive our conversations, whether we realize it or not. Aligning our thoughts and feelings with a positive frame enables generative questions to flow naturally.

In any situation, you have many possible options to pose generative questions and use positive framing. You can ask questions that generate ideas or best practices, seek clarity and understanding, solicit personal strengths, or search for times when something is working well or someone is at their best.

From everyday personal life challenges to even complex challenges at work and in communities, practicing generative questions and positive framing, informed by the AI principles, is an excellent way to sustain conversations worth having and to fuel productive and meaningful engagement.

## The Next Conversation

This book has been about choosing to increase opportunity as well as your awareness, aliveness, creativity, meaning, and joy by intentionally engaging in conversations worth having. We can do this by tuning in and intentionally using two simple practices guided by the AI principles. As David Cooperrider remarks, "It is in the depth of our connections and conversations with others that we change ourselves and our relationships, one conversation at a time."[3] In this final chapter, we emphasize the key learnings that come alive in the stories we have shared:

- Your invisible resting body-mindset heavily influences your conversations.
- Ideas, words, and actions have impact. Be mindful how you use them in your conversations so that they have a positive impact.
- Conversations create images, which in turn create the blueprint for our future. They are compelling. Create the most positive images by asking the most generative questions.

- You have many options for a conversation (critical, destructive, affirmative, and great). Choose to foster conversations worth having.
- Nothing is static. Everything is dynamic and fluid. It's not about you. And it's not about the other. Rather, it's about the intersection of the two—*the conversation*—and that can change in a heartbeat.

At times, we—the authors—still find ourselves caught up in "ain't it awful?" conversations. We still point out what's wrong with things. When we recognize what we're doing, we shake our heads and realize we are still developing these habits to induce productive and meaningful engagement. Only then can we release the self-criticism that holds us back. We encourage you to have this kind of compassion for yourself—as well as for others who join you in this adventure.

If you made it this far in the book, you know what it takes to engage in conversations worth having. Changing how you ask questions or frame situations will, of course, not happen overnight. However, with commitment and daily practice, you will experience the positive effect, and ultimately this way of being will actually become you. Committing yourself to conversations worth having will change your life, your work, and your world. These kinds of conversations have the potential to create big change—change that can influence your life *and* the world for the better.

To support your journey, we offer Conversation Bootcamps, self-directed online learning opportunities, certification, Monday Kickstarters, and a variety of products to support mastery. You can find information about these, along with our free conversation tool kit, on our website: conversationsworthhaving .today.

Our final story tells how AI can turn even the most difficult conversation into one that is worthwhile. This story was written by Jackie's daughter, Ally, and describes her experience, at the age of thirteen, shortly after the family's three-week hiking vacation was unexpectedly canceled.[4] Ally's story shows us that we can ask life-giving questions even in not-so-life-giving moments. She began:

> *Every conversation is a series of defining moments that shape and change us.*

*Things started off perfectly the day before we were to leave, except that my dad had been complaining about stomach pain. I selfishly hoped this would not affect our vacation. The afternoon before our trip, I learned how drastically wrong I was. The trip was immediately canceled.*

*My dad was diagnosed with stage four lymphoma. He had a 50 percent chance of surviving. He was in the hospital for most of the summer. My mom stayed with him the entire time. This was the first time without our parents. My younger brother, Adam, and I were shuffled from relative to relative and could only visit my dad once a week for a short amount of time.*

*I was terrified of what might happen. I had no idea what I was going to do if he was suddenly ripped away. I tried to have a brave face, but I was scared. I thought, "What if the chemotherapy won't work, and what if he dies?" I tried to push these thoughts in my mind away, but these thoughts were there all the time. During the day, I went through the motions—I smiled when people talked to me and nodded like I was listening, but I really was not there. I never heard what people said to me. I walked around appearing normal on the outside but scared and confused on the inside.*

*I remember asking my mom, "Is Dad going to die?" I wanted her to say, "No, Ally, everything will be fine." She did not; she said, "Ally, we are all going to die someday, but for now we just have to stay positive and appreciate what is." But that was it—no assurance my dad would be fine. At the time, this was hard to swallow, because all I wanted her to say was that my dad was going to be just fine. That wasn't the answer I was looking for, but, strangely, it gave me some comfort. My mom trusted me enough to tell me the truth.*

*I remember the conversation with my mom. "How can I appreciate what is? This whole situation stinks," I blurted out. "Yes, it does, honey," she responded, acknowledging my feelings. Then, my mom did what she always does when I am sad or frustrated: She changed the conversation. "Tell me about your favorite moment with your dad," she asked, as if it were the most natural question in the world. Caught off guard again for a minute, I had to stop and think. I said, "I like when Dad and I are in the kitchen baking and playing our favorite music."*

*"Ally, what else do you like most about your dad?" she asked with a heart-filled smile. That was easy. I said, "I like how he sits on the front porch with me and we watch the sun go down."*

*"Yes, I like that too," she mused. "What do you think your dad likes most about you?"*

*"I think he likes how I make him laugh," I said, smiling inwardly as I suddenly had a mental image of my dad spitting milk out of his mouth after I made him laugh.*

*"Oh, yes, he definitely likes the way you make him laugh," my mother assured me. "I'll tell you what, Ally: Tonight, I want you to sit on the porch and watch the sun go down. While you are doing that, I will push your dad up to the hospital window, and we will watch it too. This is perfect; our front porch faces east to the hospital and your dad's hospital window faces west.*

That way you can both be watching the sun set, just from different places. How does that sound?" she asked.

"Yes, Mom, I think I would like that," I answered, feeling strange that suddenly I was looking forward to the coming evening. She gave me a hug, and I watched her drive away again back to the hospital. As she drove away, I found myself smiling again, thinking about what a great conversation we had in such a bad time.

Now, as I look back on the talks we had, I realized my mom's secret formula was that she was always honest with me. She never told me "Things are going to be fine" or "It will all be back to normal soon." I knew that if my mom said it, then it was the truth and not just something to make me feel better. At first, it felt a little like this was just being positive, but then I realized these conversations were about what is, what could be, and what might be. I truly learned to focus on the things about my dad that could help him get through his treatments and regain his desire for living. Now, three years later, my dad is back at work, and we are watching the sunset from our porch again. AI helped us get through the dark moments, helping us draw on our strengths and restoring our faith. It was a lesson that was hard to grasp as a thirteen-year-old, but I was fortunate—I grew up in a household that embraced the ideals of Appreciative Inquiry for my entire life.

This experience really changed me because I learned to live with an appreciative mindset. Drawing on AI in desperate times at first did not make sense to me. I cannot tell you that I am a better person because of it, but I can tell you that I am a different person. It was a turning point for me—a time when my thinking shifted from "what about me?" to "what can I do to help my parents and others?" I learned to accept responsibility and to cope with the idea of potentially losing someone I

*will love forever. When I have to go through this again, I know*
*where and how to start the conversation.*

This story has a positive ending. Paul, her father, is doing great. He is in remission, and the life of everyone in her family has returned to a "new normal." Ally got to be a teenager again and became a most appreciative one. She learned how to handle a tough situation through the power of inquiry from an appreciative perspective. She shared:

*I learned to be appreciative, have faith, and not lose hope.*
*Today, I look at situations with an appreciative lens, which is*
*easy to do when things are going well but quite the challenge*
*when things are not. I try to see what is good and what can be*
*in just about any situation, and most of all appreciate what I*
*have.*

Ally's story illustrates how all of us can have a sense of well-being, hope, and joy even at difficult times. Appreciation and inquiry are the most essential concepts in creating powerfully positive conversations worth having. Recall the stories we have shared with you and how each person in them learned to create a positive shift. They simply practiced positive framing. The resulting conversations invited engagement and produced positive outcomes. They created environments in which people could show up as their best selves. Human systems are either degenerating or growing and evolving toward the future. Why not make it a future that has the potential to work for everyone? We are offering a simple way to do precisely that.

Writing this book has been a humbling and collaborative learning process. Most of the time, we engaged in productive and meaningful conversations about our work. There were, of course, moments when we disagreed or diverged on an idea. Tuning in and coming back to practice what we were writing about at these challenging moments proved to be an amazing experience. We discovered that it is truly delightful when something simple works so well. Plus, we have been helped immensely along our journey by engaging those in our communities: family members, Berrett-Koehler (our publisher), colleagues, and friends.

As we mentioned at the outset, we consider ourselves continuous learners in this adventure called life. We want to hear your questions, comments, thoughts, suggestions, and ideas for starting and sustaining conversations worth having in your life. Please consider joining our CWH community and visit our website, www.conversationsworthhaving.today. Join our Facebook group and share your own stories about how you are generating positive change.

There are many possible worlds out there. The probability that any one of them comes into being depends on our conversations. What kind of conversations will *you* have next?

# *Conversations Worth Having* Discussion Guide: Generative Questions for Self and Teams

Many people reach the end of this book excited to change their conversations for the better. It is going to take time and practice to create a new conversation habit. To support you, here are some journal and conversation prompts to get you started.

### Journaling: Conversations with Yourself

1. What words and behaviors foster connection for you?
2. Make a list of things that automatically trigger you. Follow with a list of some assumptions you make by completing these sentences:
   a. I believe everyone should _____.
   b. I assume _____.
   How might your assumptions be related to being triggered?
3. When triggered, what helps you tune in, open up, and become genuinely curious?
4. Reflect on a depreciative conversation you had recently (with yourself or another). What were the facts, and what did you make up or assume? If you could have that conversation again, what questions might you ask?

5. Whom or what are you avoiding, and what will happen if you don't have that conversation with them?

6. How did you use questions to shift yourself or another from a depreciative to an appreciative conversation?

7. What do you notice is happening in your relationships and your work as your ability to foster conversations worth having expands?

8. How did you flip a conversation recently? What was the impact?

9. Remember that person you've been avoiding? What questions might you ask yourself to shift the way you feel about having that conversation? How do you create a space of curiosity?

10. When are your conversations with yourself most positive and supportive? What conditions are making that possible?

## Team Conversations

1. How might we signal one another when we've just been triggered, and how might we quickly shift above the line?

2. What techniques (habits) might we try to help us tune in to ourselves and one another as a regular practice before we do anything?

3. What high-point conversations worth having did we have? What made them high-point conversations? What did we value about one another?

4. How might we build our generative question repertoire?

5. Where are we stuck? What is it we want to have happen? What questions might unstick us?

6. How might we reinforce a practice of asking great questions (and not just having answers)?

7. What can we do to acknowledge and reinforce success when it comes to how we communicate with each other?
8. What might we do to reinforce a culture of "we" instead of "me"?
9. What are we noticing about our teamwork, productivity, and engagement as a result of practicing conversations worth having?

# Notes

## Introduction

1. See Dee Hock, *One from Many: Visa and the Rise of the Chaordic Organization* (San Francisco: Berrett-Koehler, 2005). Also see M. Mitchell Waldrop, "The Trillion-Dollar Vision of Dee Hock: The Corporate Radical Who Organized Visa Wants to Dis-organize Your Company," October 31, 1996. The opening quotes come from personal conversation.

2. Peter Senge, foreword to *One from Many* by Dee Hock.

3. David Cooperrider, "The Gift of New Eyes: Personal Reflections on Appreciative Inquiry into Organizational Life," in *Research in Organizational Change and Development*, ed. Abraham B. Shani and Debra A. Noumair, vol. 25 (Bingley, UK: Emerald, 2017), 81–142.

4. In the world of Appreciative Inquiry (AI), the term *positive* means not an answer but rather a question. It invites an appreciative *search* for the true, the good, the better, and the possible—literally, everything that "gives life" and those things of value worth valuing. AI is about the search for "what gives life" to living-systems organizations, communities, industries, countries, families, networks, societies, relationships, and our global living systems when they are most alive and jointly flourishing in their inseparable and intimate interrelations. AI's generativity lies precisely in its "inquiry inspired by life" North Star and in its starting the search not in current ideals (certainties) but in the lure of unexplored possibilities (those intimations of something more) where possibility and positive potential can be sensed in the texture of the actual— searching for our world's life-giving best, in moments that are *extraordinary* (positive deviations) in moments that are *ordinary* (like Van Gogh seeing the essence in a teapot or other "ordinary" things), and even in high meaning-making moments often involving *tragedy* (see Viktor Frankl's *Man's Search for Meaning*). So when you see the word *positive*, think not of answers but of the in-depth search for what gives life, in this setting and context, something beyond our current knowledge where "inquiry is the experience of mystery, that changes our lives." Taken together, where appreciation and inquiry are wonderfully entangled, we experience knowledge that's not inert but alive, as well as an ever-expansive inauguration of our world to new possibilities.

In many ways, I've begun to question today whether there can even *be* inquiry where there is no appreciation, valuing, or amazement, or what the Greeks called *thaumazein*—the borderline between wonderment and admiration. This volume does a wonderful job of making the principles and practices of AI come alive, in easily applicable ways, thus empowering everyday vital conversation.

## Chapter 1 Shifting Conversations

1. Ironically, the first AI application was in a healthcare setting, the Cleveland Clinic Story, by David Cooperrider and Suresh Srivastva, "Appreciative Inquiry in Organizational Life," in *Research in Organizational Change and Development*, ed. W. A. Pasmore and R. Woodman, vol. 1 (Greenwich, CT: JAI Press, 1987), 129–169.

2. To learn more about Appreciative Inquiry, visit the AI Commons, https://appreciativeinquiry.champlain.edu, a worldwide portal devoted to the fullest sharing of academic resources and practical tools about Appreciative Inquiry and the rapidly growing discipline of positive change.

## Chapter 2 What Kind of Conversations Are You Having?

1. Jeffrey Ford and Laurie Ford, *The Four Conversations: Daily Communication That Gets Results* (San Francisco: Berrett-Koehler, 2009), 201. Their work focuses on four types of conversations in the workplace: initiative, understanding, performance, and closure.

2. Barbara Fredrickson, "The Role of Positive Emotions in Positive Psychology: The Broaden-and-Build Theory of Positive Emotions," *American Psychologist* 56, no. 3 (2001): 218–226.

3. Barbara Fredrickson, *Positivity: Discover the Upward Spiral That Will Change Your Life* (New York: Crown, 2009).

4. Barbara Fredrickson, *Love 2.0: How Our Supreme Emotion Affects Everything We Feel, Think, Do, and Become* (New York: Hudson Street Press, 2013).

5. Martin Seligman is a pioneer in the positive psychology field, which focuses on well-being and human flourishing. To learn more about how this field developed, visit https://www.pursuit-of-happiness.org/history-of-happiness/martin-seligman-psychology/.

6. Barbara Fredrickson, "What Good Are Positive Emotions?" *Review of General Psychology* 2, no. 30 (September 1998): 300–319.

7. A futures institute is typically a nonprofit research organization dedicated to developing practical tools, research, and programs that help people make the future—today. These institutes track signals, create maps and artifacts, and bring people together to think critically about responding in a world of continuous and rapid change. These institutes collaborate with one another, working to provide foresight for our future.

8. Gervase Bushe, "Generative Process, Generative Outcomes: The Transformational Potential of Appreciative Inquiry," in *Organizational Generativity: The Appreciative Inquiry Summit and a Scholarship of Transformation*, ed. David L. Cooperrider et al., vol. 4, *Advances in Appreciative Inquiry* (Bingley, UK: Emerald, 2013), 89–113.

9. Empirical studies confirm that this produces a positive climate and significantly higher performance. Kim Cameron, *Positive Leadership* (San Francisco:

Berrett-Koehler, 2012), and the Center for Positive Organizations; see http://positiveorgs.bus.umich.edu.

10. Examples of this are presented by Harlene Anderson, *Conversation, Language, and Possibilities: A Postmodern Approach to Therapy* (New York: Basic Books, 1997). Anderson explores the question of how therapists and clients can create relationships and conversations that allow both parties to access possibilities where none seemed to exist before. She emphasizes the importance of "therapist and client engaging in *collaborative relationships* and *generative conversations* to form *conversational partnerships* toward powerful transformations in people's lives and toward successful futures."

11. Estimates are that 80 percent of our inner dialogue is below the line. See Gilda Given, "The Power of Positive Thinking," *Medium*, June 2, 2020, https://gildagiven.medium.com/the-power-of-positive-thinking-d2f7b41c1a49; and "Self-Talk," *Psychology* Today, accessed February 15, 2021, https://www.psychologytoday.com/us/basics/self-talk.

12. Generative feedback is the practice of giving feedback in ways that help people learn and grow. "Changing Feedback from Measure & Assess to Grow & Improve with Glade Holman," interview by Lara Heacock and Kelly Stewart, *Doing (Good) Business*, podcast 73, April 19, 2021, https://www.doinggoodbusiness.com/shows/2021/4/15/73-changing-feedback-from-measure-amp-assess-to-grow-amp-improve-with-glade-holman.

Feedforward is the practice of responding to two simple questions: What resonates (what do I like)? and What suggestions do I have to make it even better? Marshall Goldsmith first coined this term to encourage people to ask others for ways to improve their performance. The point is to offer suggestions about the future instead of criticism about the past. Marshall Goldsmith with Mark Reiter, *What Got You Here Won't Get You There: How Successful People Become Even More Successful!* (New York: Hyperion, 2007).

13. Marilee Adams has written two books on question thinking. She proposes two paradigms of questioning—the judger and the learner—and details how best to shift from the judger paradigm to the learner paradigm. For further reading, see Marilee Adams, *Change Your Questions, Change Your Life: 12 Powerful Tools for Leadership, Coaching, and Life*, 3rd ed. (Oakland: Berrett-Koehler, 2016), and also her first book, *The Art of the Question: A Guide to Short-Term Question-Centered Therapy* (New York: Wiley, 1998).

14. Joe Hirsch, *The Feedback Fix: Dump the Past, Embrace the Future, and Lead the Way to Change* (Lanham, MD: Rowman & Littlefield, 2017).

15. Barbara Fredrickson's research indicates that we need a minimum of a 3:1 ratio of positive emotions to negative emotions in order to stay healthy and vital. Fredrickson, *Positivity*. Marcial Losada and Emily Heaphy's research shows that high-performing teams actually have a 6:1 ratio: "The Role of Positivity and Connectivity in the Performance of Business Teams: A Nonlinear Dynamics Model," *American Behavioral Scientist* 47, no. 6 (February 2004): 740–765.

16. Barbara Fredrickson, "The Value of Positive Emotions," *American Scientist* 91, no. 4 (2003): 330–334.

17. Losada and Heaphy, "The Role of Positivity and Connectivity"; and John Gottman, *Why Marriages Succeed or Fail* (New York: Simon & Schuster, 1994).

## Chapter 3 Who's Driving? Tune In

1. Doc Childre et al., *Heart Intelligence, Connecting with the Intuitive Guidance of the Heart* (Boulder Creek, CA: HeartMath, 2016).
2. Carol Dweck, *Mindset: The New Psychology of Success* (New York: Ballantine, 2016).
3. To deepen your appreciation of the power of locating yourself, watch a three-and-a-half minute video created by the Conscious Leadership Group, https://www.youtube.com/watch?v=fLqzYDZAqCI.
4. Andrew Huberman, neuroscientist and head of Madefor Advisory Board, Madefor's member communication, January 20, 2021, https://www.getmadefor.com; and Jessica Wapner, "Vision and Breathing May Be the Secrets to Surviving 2020," *Scientific American*, November 16, 2020, https://www.scientificamerican.com/article/vision-and-breathing-may-be-the-secrets-to-surviving-2020.
5. Huberman, Madefor's member communications.
6. Viktor Frankl, *Man's Search for Meaning* (Boston: Beacon Press, 2006, orig. publ. 1959).
7. We offer Conversation Bootcamps to support the practice of conversations worth having. Visit our website to learn more: https://conversationsworthhaving.today.

## Chapter 4 Two Simple Appreciative Practices

1. Gervase Bushe, "Generative Process, Generative Outcomes: The Transformational Potential of Appreciative Inquiry," in *Organizational Generativity: The Appreciative Inquiry Summit and a Scholarship of Transformation*, ed. David L. Cooperrider et al., vol. 4, *Advances in Appreciative Inquiry* (Bingley, UK: Emerald, 2013), 89–113.
2. Gretchen Spreitzer and Scott Sonenshein define a *positive deviance* as something that represents "intentional behaviors that depart from the norm of a reference group in honorable ways." Thus, it reaches a "level of positive deviance that extends beyond achieving effectiveness or ordinary success (p. 209); see "Positive Deviance and Extraordinary Organizing," in *Positive Organizational Scholarship: Foundations of a New Discipline,* ed. Kim S. Cameron, Jane E. Dutton, and Robert E. Quinn (San Francisco: Berrett-Koehler, 2003), 207–224.
3. Chip Heath and Dan Heath, *Switch: How to Change Things When Change Is Hard* (New York: Broadway Books, 2010).
4. For more information on transformative talk about how to reflect and reframe with positive intent, see Robert J. Marshak, "Generative Conversations: How to Use Deep Listening and Transforming Talk in Coaching and Consulting," *OD Practitioner* 36, no. 3 (2004): 25–29.
5. Barbara Fredrickson, "The Value of Positive Emotions," *American Scientist* 91, no. 4 (2003): 330–334.
6. Gervase Bushe, "Appreciative Inquiry Is Not (Just) about the Positive," *OD Practitioner* 39, no. 4 (2007): 30–35.
7. The term *flip* has been used by many to describe how to shift from negative to positive. Thomas H. White, former president of GTE Telephone Operations, referenced the "flip-side of the coin" when describing using AI in his organization in David L. Cooperrider, Diana Whitney, and Jacqueline M. Stavros, *Appreciative Inquiry Handbook* (Bedford Heights, OH: Lakeshore, 2003), xx.

Diana Whitney, Amanda Trosten-Bloom, and Kae Rader describe "the flip" in *Appreciative Leadership* (San Francisco: McGraw-Hill, 2010), 35–41, and Jeremy McCarthy refers to "the positive flip" in *The Psychology of Wellbeing* blog, http://psychologyofwellbeing.com. Over the years, this shift has been referred to as "the flip" in the AI community or "the positive flip" in the positive psychology community.

## Chapter 5 What's Fueling Your Conversations?

1. Under the guidance of Suresh Srivastva, David Cooperrider created the original AI principles. These principles were first published by Cooperrider and Srivastva in "Appreciative Inquiry in Organizational Life," *Research in Organization Change and Development,* ed. W. A. Pasmore and R. Woodman, vol. 1 (Greenwich, CT: JAI Press, 1987), 129–169.

2. For a deeper dive into the AI principles and how they govern and affect our action and relationships, see Jacqueline M. Stavros and Cheri Torres, *Dynamic Relationships: Unleashing the Power of Appreciative Inquiry in Daily Living* (Chagrin Falls, OH: Taos Institute, 2005).

3. For more detailed information on AI systematic discovery of what gives life to a system, see David Cooperrider, Diana Whitney, and Jacqueline M. Stavros, *The Appreciative Inquiry Handbook*, 2nd ed. (San Francisco: Berrett-Koehler, 2008).

4. By *constructionist* we are referring to social constructionism, which is a theory of knowledge grounded in the idea that we jointly (that is, socially) construct meaning and understanding about the world based on our experience and shared assumptions. We create models of the social world, then we share and reify those models through language. The foremost leaders in social constructionist theory and practice are members of the Taos Institute. You will find further information and resources at https://www.taosinstitute.net.

5. Ropes courses, also called challenge courses, comprise a set of activities that require significant teamwork and shared leadership for success. Typically, these courses are built in the woods. Outward Bound popularized such courses.

6. Cheri Torres, *The Appreciative Facilitator: A Handbook for Facilitators and Teachers* (Asheville, NC: Collaborative by Design, 2001).

7. The Poetic Principle says, "Our lives are like an open book or a poem [that] is constantly being written, and rewritten, read and reinterpreted. We can find new meaning in old story lines when we ask different questions." In Stavros and Torres, *Dynamic Relationships*, 65–66.

8. David L. Cooperrider, "Positive Image, Positive Action: The Affirmative Basis of Organizing," in *Appreciative Management and Leadership,* ed. Suresh Srivastva and David L. Cooperrider, rev. ed. (Euclid, OH: Williams Custom, 1999), 91–125.

## Chapter 6 Scaling Up Great Conversations

1. Visit the AI Commons to see illustrations of cities, countries, organizations, and global initiatives around the world that use the AI 5-D Cycle: https://appreciativeinquiry.champlain.edu.

2. To learn more about the Fairmount Santrol story, visit www.youtube.com/watch?v=eGOvgFoDZaY.

3. Jennifer Deckard, "How Appreciative Inquiry Contributes to a Culture of Do Good, Do Well," (keynote speech, Flourishing Conference, Cleveland, OH, June 16, 2017).

4. For more in-depth information about the AI 5-D Cycle in organizations, see Diana Whitney and Amanda Trosten-Bloom, *The Power of Appreciative Inquiry: A Practical Guide to Positive Change* (San Francisco: Berrett-Koehler, 2003), and David L. Cooperrider, Diana Whitney, and Jacqueline M. Stavros, *The Appreciative Inquiry Handbook,* 2nd ed. (San Francisco: Berrett-Koehler, 2008).

5. For more information on using AI to create strategy and strategic plans, see Jacqueline M. Stavros and Gina Hinrichs, *The Thin Book of SOAR: Creating Strategy That Inspires Innovation and Engagement,* 2nd ed. (Bend, OR: Thin Book, 2019), or visit https://www.soar-strategy.com.

## Chapter 7 It's Not Magic, It's Science!

1. Margaret Wheatley, *Leadership and the New Science: Discovering Order in a Chaotic World* (San Francisco: Berrett-Koehler, 2006); and David Rock, *Your Brain at Work: Strategies for Overcoming Distraction, Regaining Focus, and Working Smarter All Day Long* (New York: Harper Business, 2020).

2. *Positive psychology* is defined as "the scientific study of what makes life worth living." Christopher Peterson, "What Is Positive Psychology and What Is It Not?" *Psychology Today* (May 16, 2008), https://www.psychologytoday.com /blog/the-good-life/200805/what-is-positive-psychology-and-what-is-it-not. It is further defined as "the scientific study of positive human functioning and flourishing on multiple levels that include the biological, personal, relational, institutional, cultural, and global dimensions of life." Martin Seligman and Mihaly Csikszentmihalyi, "Positive Psychology: An Introduction," *American Psychologist* 55, no. 1 (2000): 5–14.

3. David Cooperrider, "The Concentration Effect of Strengths: How the Whole System AI Summits Bring Out the Best in Human Enterprise," *Organizational Dynamics* 41, no. 2 (2012): 106–117.

4. University of California, Los Angeles, "New UCLA Imaging Study First to Show Placebo Alters Brain Function in Individuals with Major Depression," *ScienceDaily*, January 2, 2002, https://www.sciencedaily.com/releases/2002 /01/020102074543.htm.

5. One example of HeartMath's work with law enforcement over the last twenty-five years is Judith P. Andersen et al., "Applying Resilience Promotion Training among Special Forces Police Officers," *SAGE Open* 5, no. 2 (April–June 2015): 1–8, https://doi.org/10.1177/2158244015590446.

6. Doc Childre and Howard Martin, *The HeartMath Solution* (New York: Harper Collins, 1999).

7. Childre and Martin.

8. David L. Cooperrider, "Positive Image, Positive Action: The Affirmative Basis of Organizing," in *Appreciative Management and Leadership,* ed. Suresh Srivastva and David L. Cooperrider, rev. ed. (Euclid, OH: Williams Custom, 1999), 93–95, 106.

9. Tania Lombrozo, "The Truth about the Right Brain/Left Brain Relationship," December 2, 2013, https://www.npr.org/sections/13.7/2013/12/02/248089436

/the-truth-about-the-left-brain-right-brain-relationship; and Evelyn Virschup and Bernard Virschup, "Visual Imagery: The Language of the Right Brain," *in Imagery: Its Many Dimensions and Applications,* ed. Joseph E. Shorr et al. (New York: Springer, 1980).

10. Daniel S. Kirschenbaum et al., "Effects of Differential Self-Monitoring and Level of Mastery on Sports Performance: Brain Power Bowling," *Cognitive Therapy and Research* 6, no, 3 (1982): 335–342.

11. Cooperrider, "Positive Image, Positive Action," 109.

12. Cooperrider, "Positive Image, Positive Action," 95–96; and "The Power of the Placebo Effect," *Harvard Health Publishing,* updated August 9, 2019, https://www.health.harvard.edu/mental-health/the-power-of-the-placebo-effect.

13. Robert Rosenthal, "Interpersonal Expectancy Effects: A 30-Year Perspective," *Current Directions in Psychological Sciences* 3, no. 6 (December 1994): 176–179; and Jane Elliott, "A Class Divided," *PBS Frontline,* March 26, 1985, https://www.pbs.org/wgbh/pages/frontline/shows/divided.

14. Cooperrider, "Positive Image, Positive Action," 92–102.

15. Peale was a hugely influential popularizer of the power of positive thinking in the United States. Ziglar was a highly successful salesperson, motivational speaker, and trainer; he wrote more than twelve books and influenced the lives of millions of people with his positive messages and encouraging words.

16. Barbara Fredrickson, "The Role of Positive Emotions in Positive Psychology: The Broaden-and-Build Theory of Positive Emotions," *American Psychologist* 56, no. 3 (2001): 218–226.

17. Frederickson, 218–226.

18. Barbara Fredrickson, *Positivity: Discover the Upward Spiral That Will Change Your Life* (New York: Crown, 2009).

19. Barbara Fredrickson, *Love 2.0: How Our Supreme Emotion Affects Everything We Feel, Think, Do, and Become* (New York: Hudson Street Press, 2013).

20. Marcial Losada and Emily Heaphy, "The Role of Positivity and Connectivity in the Performance of Business Teams: A Nonlinear Dynamics Model," *American Behavioral Scientist* 47, no. 6 (February 2004): 740–765.

21. John Gottman, *Why Marriages Succeed or Fail* (New York: Simon & Schuster, 1994).

22. Gottman.

23. For a brief but complete overview of the history of positive psychology, see Reham Al Taher, "The 5 Founding Fathers and a History of Positive Psychology," *PositivePsychology.com,* December 10, 2020, https://positivepsychologyprogram.com/founding-fathers.

24. Martin Seligman, *Flourish: A Visionary New Understanding of Happiness and Well-Being* (New York: Free Press, 2011), 13.

25. Seligman, 16–18.

26. Cooperrider, "The Concentration Effect of Strengths."

## Chapter 8 Any Time, Any Place, Any Situation

1. Jane Watkins was instrumental in bringing AI into organization life in hundreds of organizations in more than fifty countries. Jane Magruder Watkins, Bernard Mohr, and Ralph Kelly, *Appreciative Inquiry: Change at the Speed of Imagination,* 2nd ed. (San Francisco: Pfeiffer, 2011).

2. Neil Samuels and Cheri Torres, in collaboration with the Appreciative Governance Team, "Organizational Design Principles for Appreciative Governance," *AI Practitioner* 13, no. 4 (November 2011): 24.

3. Jacqueline M. Stavros and Cherri Torres, *Dynamic Relationships: Unleashing the Power of Appreciative Inquiry in Daily Living* (Chagrin Falls, OH: Taos Institute, 2005), 15.

4. This original, full story by Ally is in the issue Young Practitioners, Co-Creating the Future of Appreciative Inquiry, "Learning to Leverage Appreciative Inquiry in a Not So Appreciative Moment," *Appreciative Inquiry Practitioner* 19, no. 1 (February 2017). It has been abridged here and updated by Ally as she recalls the conversation she had using AI in a difficult situation.

# Selected Bibliography

This list includes the books that were useful to us in writing this work. It is not a complete record of all the works and sources we consulted; it is included as a resource for those who wish to pursue further study on the topics addressed in this book.

Adams, Marilee. *Change Your Questions, Change Your Life: 12 Powerful Tools for Leadership, Coaching, and Life.* 3rd ed. Oakland: Berrett-Koehler, 2016.

Barrett, Frank J., and Ronald E. Fry. *Appreciative Inquiry: A Positive Approach to Building Cooperative Capacity.* Chagrin Falls, OH: Taos Institute, 2005.

Cooperrider, David L., and Diana Whitney. *Appreciative Inquiry: A Positive Revolution in Change.* San Francisco: Berrett-Koehler, 2005.

Cooperrider, David L., Diana Whitney, and Jacqueline M. Stavros. *Appreciative Inquiry Handbook.* 2nd ed. San Francisco: Berrett-Koehler, 2008.

Dweck, Carol. *Mindset: The New Psychology of Success.* New York: Ballantine, 2016.

Ford, Jeffrey, and Laurie Ford. *The Four Conversations: Daily Communication That Gets Results.* San Francisco: Berrett-Koehler, 2009.

Frankl, Viktor. *Man's Search for Meaning.* Boston: Beacon Press, 2006. Orig. publ. 1959.

Fredrickson, Barbara. *Positivity: Discover the Upward Spiral That Will Change Your Life.* New York: Crown, 2009.

Fredrickson, Barbara. *Love 2.0: How Our Supreme Emotion Affects Everything We Feel, Think, Do, and Become.* New York: Hudson Street Press, 2013.

Hammond, Sue Annis. *The Thin Book of Appreciative Inquiry.* Bend, OR: Thin Book, 2013.

Ludema, James D., Diana Whitney, Bernard J. Mohr, and Thomas J. Griffin. *The Appreciative Inquiry Summit: A Practitioner's Guide for Leading Large-Group Change.* San Francisco: Berrett-Koehler, 2003.

McArthur-Blair, Joan, and Jeanie Cockell. *Building Resilience with Appreciative Inquiry: A Leadership Journey through Hope, Despair, and Forgiveness.* Oakland, CA: Berrett-Koehler, 2018.

Rock, David. *Your Brain at Work: Strategies for Overcoming Distraction, Regaining Focus, and Working Smarter All Day Long.* New York: HarperBusiness, 2020.

Seligman, Martin. *Flourish: A Visionary New Understanding of Happiness and Well-Being.* New York: Free Press, 2011.

Srivastva, Suresh, and David L. Cooperrider. *Appreciative Management and Leadership: The Power of Positive Thought and Action in Organizations.* Rev. ed. Euclid, OH: Williams Custom, 1999.

Stavros, Jacqueline M., and Gina Hinrichs. *The Thin Book of SOAR: Creating Strategy That Inspires Innovation and Engagement.* 2nd ed. Bend, OR: Thin Book, 2019.

Stavros, Jacqueline M., and Cheri Torres. *Dynamic Relationships: Unleashing the Power of Appreciative Inquiry in Daily Living.* Chagrin Falls, OH: Taos Institute, 2005.

Thatchenkery, Tojo, and Carol Metzker. *Appreciative Intelligence: Seeing the Mighty Oak in the Acorn.* San Francisco: Berrett-Koehler, 2006.

Torres, Cheri. *The Appreciative Facilitator: A Handbook for Facilitators and Teachers.* Asheville, NC: Collaborative by Design, 2001.

Watkins, Jane Magruder, Bernard Mohr, and Ralph Kelly. *Appreciative Inquiry: Change at the Speed of Imagination.* 2nd ed. San Francisco: Pfeiffer, 2011.

Whitney, Diana, and Amanda Trosten-Bloom. *The Power of Appreciative Inquiry: A Practical Guide to Positive Change.* San Francisco: Berrett-Koehler, 2003.

# Acknowledgments

No book is the result of its authors alone, and ours is no different. Writing *Conversations Worth Having* emerged from conversation after conversation with one another and with our families, colleagues, friends, editor, and clients, many of whose stories we tell in these pages. We would be remiss if we did not acknowledge our twenty years of friendship with each other and the complementary nature of our styles and temperaments, which brought balance and clarity to our collective writing. Our understanding of just how simple it is to engage in great conversations unveiled itself as we wrote. The foundation for our work, of course, is grounded in the brilliance and generosity of David Cooperrider, Ron Fry, and their colleagues at Case Western Reserve University. They have given a gift to the world that has blessed our lives and careers. A special thank-you to David for writing the introduction—we are humbled and inspired by your words.

We also acknowledge, greatly appreciate, and thank other members of the AI community who helped shape our understanding and practical application of Appreciative Inquiry: Frank Barrett, Gervase Bushe, Jeanie Cockell, Dawn Dole-Cooperrider, Lindsey Godwin, Sue Hammond, Colette

Herrick, Ralph Kelly, Sallie Lee, Jane Magruder-Watkins, Joan McArthur-Blair, Mo McKenna, Bernard Mohr, Anne Radford, Dan Saint, Neil Samuels, Marge Schiller, David Shaked, Robyn Stratton-Berkessel, Amanda Trosten-Bloom, Diana Whitney, and Joep de Yong. As well, we thank Ken Gergen and the Taos Institute associates for their commitment to the field of social construction and their efforts to bring its application to the world.

A special thanks to those we work with for all the many conversations worth having we've had over the years, which no doubt contributed to what appears in these pages: the leadership at the Center for Appreciative Inquiry/Company of Experts (Kathy Becker, Jim Pulliam, and Melissa Robaina); those at the Cooperrider Center for Appreciative Inquiry (Lindsey Godwin, Jessica Blackman, and Alyssa Labare); members of Innovation Partners International (Mike Feinson, Lisa Hirsh, Bob Laliberte, Ada Jo Mann, Christine Whitney Sanchez, and Bill Scott); Colette Herrick of Insight Shift; the team at XCHANGE: Conversations for Exponential Outcomes (Jon Berghoff, Scot Lowry, and Laura MacMinn); Tony and Jen Silbert of Spartina; and members of NextMove (Haiz Oppenheimer and Amelia Terrapin).

We are grateful to everyone who has attended our Conversation Bootcamps, helping us learn better ways of teaching and applying these practices. And we deeply appreciate those who have contributed much of their precious time, creativity, and wisdom, influencing our thinking, training, and diverse programs and products to support making these practices common nature. These include Toni Benner, Deb Connors, Michael Emmart, Elle Finnegan, Fasiha Haq, Deb Maher, Lauren Rayburn, Lisa Schmith, Kelly Stewart, Laura Torres, Sylvette Wake, Elizabeth Warner, and Lyn Williams. Also, special acknowledgment to Ethan and Grant Webster for creating the CWH jingle; have a listen on our website.

Along the way, we have had countless conversations about the book with others. They offered words of encouragement as well as valuable insights and feedback that helped shape our writing. These others include the Lawrence Technological University family of administration, staff, faculty, and students; the positive psychology and positivity community; the Center for Positive Organizations; Tammy Love and staff members at the Institute of Nuclear Power Operations; the Reverend Sally Beth Shore and members of the Unitarian Universalist Church of Spartanburg, South Carolina; and Amy Climer for her insight on our new graphic for the nature of conversations. We are also deeply grateful to Sandra Grace, who saw the potential for this book to impact the world. Her generosity in giving our book to others and connecting us with resources and speaking engagements has been appreciated.

We are also grateful to our clients, colleagues, friends, and family members for the stories that appear in the book. We have changed most of your names, but you no doubt recognized yourself in your story. Thank you for being an example and for sharing your story with us so that we can share it with others.

We would especially like to thank the members of our newest family—Berrett-Koehler Publishers (BK). Named in the order in which we met them, we are deeply grateful to Jeevan Sivasubramaniam for his endless patience and for opening the door into BK. He waited many years until it was the right moment for our manuscript to come together. We love his thoughtful directness, sense of humor, and responsiveness.

We express gratitude also to Steve Piersanti, our editor, without whom this book would not be in your hands.

His awareness of the power and impact that Appreciative Inquiry can have in the world made his work with us all the more potent. His knowledge and expertise, coupled with his thought-provoking questions, helped us simplify our message. We greatly appreciate his willingness to push back and then let us sit with ambiguity until we found our way to clarifying complex AI concepts.

We sincerely appreciate the time, care, and incredibly helpful recommendations given to us from our BK manuscript reviewers: Julie Clayton, Bette Krakau, Carol Metzker, and Chloe Park. Each made valuable contributions to the final manuscript. In addition, we are grateful for the time and editorial support given by Cecile Betit, Dan Casetta, Matthew Cole, and Edward Kimball. A special thank-you to Mark Levy for his inspiration, his writing tips, and the enthusiasm he continuously brought to our conversations.

We are grateful to the more than five hundred people who gave us feedback on the book's title, making it very clear that *Conversations Worth Having* was a winner. Many thanks to Lasell Whipple and her production team; designing the original cover was easy, thanks to Lasell and Adam Johnson, who translated our conversations about the cover into a vibrant, colorful design for the first edition. Thank you to the production team in the second edition: Edward Wade and Valerie Caldwell. Our gratitude to Steven Hiatt, our text designer, and to Sharon Goldinger and the editors at PeopleSpeak for book production, copy editing, and proofreading. And much appreciation for Courtney Schonfeld and Tiffany Williams for making the audio version of our book available.

Our publishing family continued to grow as we met and collaborated with the remarkable and detail-focused marketing team. Much gratitude and appreciation for our team lead, Mike Crowley, as well as for María Jesús Aguiló, Shabnam Banerjee-McFarland, Leslie Crandell, Sohayla Farman, Kristen Frantz, David Marshall, Liz McKellar, Katie Sheehan, Mayowa Tomori, and Johanna Vondeling. Thank you for bringing the message in this book to the world. And a note of thanks to the BK Authors Group for providing workshops that enliven, uplift, and energize the BK author community. We are grateful to have the opportunity to connect with other authors and thankful for their support. We are thrilled to be part of this community, and we commit to the same generosity we have been shown.

We are honored to be a part of the BK family, aligning our words and work with their mission: *to create a world that works for all!* We are so grateful to be on this journey at this time in history with an organization as honorable as BK.

In closing, we express our gratitude for our families. Special thanks to our husbands, Paul Stavros and Michael Torres, who are loving, supportive, and encouraging even when writing takes over our evenings and weekends. An extra note of gratitude to Paul for his enthusiasm and design efforts.

We are also deeply aware of how much our children have provided us opportunities to learn and to practice generative questions and positive framing, and to come up against the principles time and time again. They have kept us honest by asking generative questions when we were focused on what's wrong, reminding us to look for what is *right* with the world. Huge thank-yous to Ally, for her constant cheer and life-defining story in our final chapter, and to Adam, for his sense of humor and ability to take care of himself when writing consumed our time. Laura and Carmen, we are grateful for your encouragement, your joy in hearing about our work, and your reflection of all that is good, true, and beautiful in the world. To all of our children: We hope the conversations taking place in the world today begin to transform into conversations that generate a greener, more loving, inclusive, and human world that is safe and enlivening for you and *your* children—and your children's children for seven generations to come.

# Index

Page references followed by *f* indicate an illustrated figure; those followed by *t* indicate a table.

# CWH Offerings

Thank you for taking the time to read our book. Though the practices are simple, we know shifting our habits of conversation is not easy. There are numerous ways to deepen your practice of generative questions and positive framing as well as ways to get involved with those of us working to create a worldwide movement to generate positive change, one conversation at a time. The following programs and products make it fun and easier to create a habit of fostering conversations worth having.

### Conversation Bootcamps

The Conversation Bootcamp is designed to build your capacity to intentionally foster conversations worth having through experiential activities and regular daily practice. The Strategic Conversations Bootcamp builds your capacity to engage everyone in strategic conversations that increase productivity and performance, reduce costs and conflicts, and improve customer service at all levels. The bootcamps are offered online, in person, and as self-directed online programs.

### Trainer Certification (Train-the-Trainer)

Our certification program is an intensive, experiential learning opportunity that combines the theory, practice, and research of Appreciative Inquiry, positive psychology, and neuroscience to support trainers and practitioners interested in bringing these communication practices to their organizations and clients. Certified trainers/practitioners come from a broad spectrum of fields, including human resources, business and industry, education and teaching, social work, healthcare, equity and social justice, nonprofit leadership, and government.

### The Focus Book Series

The short books in the Focus Book Series concentrate on applying the practices within a specific context (e.g., self-talk, healthcare, well-being, education, parenting, youth). They provide stories and applications relevant to the specific focus. Visit our website for a growing list of these books.

### Monday Kickstarters

Practice flipping problems into positive frames and asking generative questions. These live thirty-minute four-week sessions occur throughout the year. Sessions are recorded and available on our Vimeo channel. You can also read the outcomes on our blog.

### Supporting Products

We believe learning should be fun and experiential. Check back routinely for new products to support learning. Download our conversation tool kits. Use our decks of question cards, games, posters, and journals to make practice and developing new habits fun and sticky!

Learn more at our website:
https://conversationsworthhaving.today

Join the movement!
#ConversationsWorthHaving

# Collaborative Partnerships

Our dream is to create a worldwide movement of conversations worth having, resulting in a groundswell of innovation and systems change that generates a world that works for all people. This demands collaboration. If you are interested in being a part of that change, we encourage you to attend one of our Conversation Bootcamps, become a certified (CHW) trainer/practitioner, and learn more about each of our partner organizations.

### The Cooperrider Center for Appreciative Inquiry

The David L. Cooperrider Center for Appreciative Inquiry is the global Center of Excellence for Appreciative Inquiry and strengths-based management practices. The center is the first academic-based center focusing on advancing the theory and practice of Appreciative Inquiry. Its mission is to educate leaders to be the best *in* the world at seeing the best *for* the world, as well as to discover and design positive institutions, organizations, and communities that elevate, magnify, and bring our highest human strengths to the practice of positive organization development and change. Check out the AI Commons. Visit champlain.edu/appreciativeinquiry.

## The Center for Appreciative Inquiry

The Center for Appreciative Inquiry (CAI) has dedicated itself to creating positive and innovative change at all systems' levels. Its philosophy for sustainable change stems from the belief that every human possesses incomprehensible value. Through the art of positive inquiry, CAI helps individuals, groups, and organizations connect with their existing talents, strengths, and resources to create shared visions of the future that are inclusive, creative, and provoke action. As leaders in Appreciative Inquiry trainings and certifications, we meet the rapidly changing needs of leaders in today's global economy by continuously delivering workshops and certification courses that invite conversation, foster inclusivity, nurture creativity, and inspire action. Visit centerforappreciativeinquiry.net.

# About the Authors

**Jackie Stavros, DM.** Jackie's passion is working with others to discover their purpose in creating positive change. She is recognized for her creation of SOAR, a positive approach to strategic thinking, planning, conversations, and leading that focuses on strengths, opportunities, aspirations, and results  (www.soar-strategy.com). She has over thirty years of leadership, strategy, organization development, and change management experience. The heart of her work is using Appreciative Inquiry (AI), one of the most popular approaches to positive change, which brings out the best in people to impact productivity, engagement, and performance in their organizations and communities. Jackie has been integrating strengths-based approaches into her research, teaching, training, coaching, and consulting work to strengthen relationships and inspire innovation. She works with organizations in leadership development, team building, and strategic planning. She helps them identify and articulate their values, vision, mission, strategy, and initiatives to build collaborative teams and communities. She has worked across all sectors, including for-profit, non-profit, government, and a wide spectrum of industries.

Jackie is a professor at Lawrence Technological University (LTU) College of Business and IT in Michigan. She is a member of the AI Council of Practitioners for the Cooperrider Center for Appreciative Inquiry and the Taos Institute. She serves as an AI Mentor for XCHANGE: Conversations for Exponential Outcomes. Before she joined LTU, her industry work included manufacturing, automotive, banking, technology, government, and professional services. Her first professional position was as a sales rep for Cutco Cutlery, whose leaders planted in her a seed of positivity.

Jackie has coauthored many books and articles, including *Appreciative Inquiry Handbook: For Leaders of Change* and *The Thin Book of SOAR: Creating Strategy That Inspires Innovation and Engagement*. Her work has been featured in *Forbes*, *SmartBrief*, Detroit's *Live in the D*, and *DBusiness Magazine*. She has presented her research and work in over twenty-five countries. She is a keynote speaker on AI, SOAR, and positive approaches to leadership development and change. Jackie earned a DM (doctorate in management) from Case Western Reserve University, an MBA from Michigan State University, and a BA from Wayne State University. She lives in Brighton, Michigan, with her husband, Paul, and loveable dog, Rex.

jackiestavros.com

jackie@ConversationsWorthHaving.today

**Cheri B. Torres, PhD.** As lead catalyst at Collaborative by Design, Cheri partners with people to catalyze positive change in workplaces and communities. The two simple practices she introduces give leaders and teams the power to strengthen relationships, expand possibilities,  and increase productivity and engagement through everyday conversation. These practices are grounded in neuroscience, positive psychology, and Appreciative Inquiry, one of the most widely used approaches for systems change. She's worked with thousands of leaders and teams around the world to support high performance, engagement, culture transformation, and organization success. She also partners with communities and organizations for whole-system change and strategic planning, bringing all stakeholders together for planning, design, and collaborative action. She has worked across all sectors: corporate, government, education, and social profit/NGOs, online and in person, supporting their capacity for learning and innovation, shared leadership, teamwork, and collective impact. She has trained thousands of trainers and teachers around the world in the use and practice of Experiential Learning, Appreciative Inquiry, and other strengths-based processes.

A perpetual learner, she's accumulated a PhD in educational psychology with a specialization in collaborative learning, an MBA, a master's in transpersonal psychology, Level 2 certification in the Barrett Values Culture Transformation Tools, and Level II certification in Spiral Dynamics Integral.

She has authored numerous books and articles, including *The Appreciative Facilitator: Accelerated Learning Practice, From Conflict to Collaboration,* and *Dynamic Relationships: Unleashing the Power of Appreciative Inquiry in Daily Living.* She's been featured in leading media sources including *Fast Company, Forbes, HR Magazine, SmartBrief, Training Industry,* and *Training Magazine.* Her keynote presentations reach a broad range of people, including HR directors, organization development practitioners, women leaders, youth prevention specialists, educators, and individual social profit organizations and corporations. She codesigned and patented Mobile Team Challenge, an award-winning portable low-ropes course. She lives in Asheville, North Carolina, with her husband, Michael; their dog, Annabel; and Ziggy-cat.

cheritorres.com

cheri@ConversationsWorthHaving.today

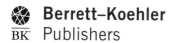

Dear reader,

Thank you for picking up this book and welcome to the worldwide BK community! You're joining a special group of people who have come together to create positive change in their lives, organizations, and communities.

## What's BK all about?

Our mission is to connect people and ideas to create a world that works for all.

Why? Our communities, organizations, and lives get bogged down by old paradigms of self-interest, exclusion, hierarchy, and privilege. But we believe that can change. That's why we seek the leading experts on these challenges—and share their actionable ideas with you.

## A welcome gift

To help you get started, we'd like to offer you a **free copy** of one of our bestselling ebooks:

### www.bkconnection.com/welcome

When you claim your **free ebook**, you'll also be subscribed to our blog.

## Our freshest insights

Access the best new tools and ideas for leaders at all levels on our blog at ideas.bkconnection.com.

Sincerely,

Your friends at Berrett-Koehler

Certified

Corporation